**DEDICATED TO THE MARINES AND SAILORS
KILLED IN BEIRUT, LEBANON, 1982-1984.**

Many Marines helped to make this book a reality. To thank and honor them and their Corps, which takes pride in taking care of its own, part of the proceeds of the sale of this book are being donated to the Marine Corps Scholarship Foundation, for the children of those who fell in Lebanon.

(Overleaf, pages 2-3) Split-second coordination between air support, artillery, infantry, and heavy armor, like the M-60 tank, gives the U.S. Marine Corps a fighting edge. Young lieutenants learn the skills to lead Marines in battle during a three-day "war" at The Basic School, Quantico, Virginia. (Overleaf, pages 4-5) A Marine supply clerk and cook refine close-combat skills. Every Marine is a rifleman and a warrior first, regardless of his or her military occupation. Combat skills are reviewed frequently. "When the chips are down, the cooks and bakers have to pick up a rifle and do their duty as Marines," says an officer. (Overleaf, pages 6-7) The awesome firepower of a Marine infantry company drops a curtain of lead on an advancing "Soviet" motorized rifle battalion in a night exercise. (Overleaf, pages 8-9) Dress-blue uniform with, left to right, the Navy Commendation Medal, Good Conduct Medal, National Defense Service Medal, Vietnam Service Medal, and Republic of Vietnam Campaign Medal. (Above) One of the handpicked Marine security guards at the U.S. Embassy, Rome, Italy. Marines have been protecting U.S. legations since the Boxer Rebellion in China in 1900.

Designed by Marilyn F. Appleby.
Edited by Ross A. Howell Jr., Kathleen D. Valenzi,
Marlessa K. Knoles, and Mary S. Coryell.
Photographs and text copyright © 1988 by Agostino von Hassell.
All rights reserved.
Foreword copyright © 1988 by Bernard E. Trainor. All rights reserved.
This book, or any portions thereof, may not be reproduced
or transmitted in any form or by any means, electronic or mechanical,
including photocopying, recording, or by any information storage and
retrieval system, without permission in writing from the publisher.
Photography and text may not be reproduced without permission of Agostino von Hassell.
Foreword may not be reproduced without permission of Bernard E. Trainor.
Library of Congress Catalog Card Number 88-80089
ISBN 0-943231-08-6
Printed and bound in Japan by Dai Nippon Printing Co., Ltd.
Published by Howell Press, Inc., 2000 Holiday Drive,
Charlottesville, Virginia 22901. Telephone (804) 977-4006.
First printing

HOWELL PRESS

WARRIORS
THE UNITED STATES MARINES

PHOTOGRAPHY AND TEXT BY AGOSTINO VON HASSELL WITH KEITH CROSSLEY

FOREWORD BY BERNARD TRAINOR

CONTENTS

Each silver ring of the staff bearing the Marine Corps colors is engraved with the names of past battles.

A grunt encounters a water obstacle. "The Corps will stretch your abilities to the limit and beyond," yells a drill instructor at Parris Island, South Carolina.

FOREWORD

Crusades are noble events. World War II was a crusade. I missed it by nine months and was sorely disappointed. The war dominated the news throughout my high-school years and was a passion for my schoolmates and me. We thrilled to the headlines of Americans bombing the Ruhr and Marines landing on remote islands like Tarawa and Guam. We could hardly wait for graduation to join our older brothers and prove our mettle in battle.

Patriotic teen-agers must have been the only group in the United States unhappy to see the war end in September 1945. Wars never reached the same noble heights in subsequent years, but we fought them anyway.

For me, there was never a doubt that I would be a Marine. I would go into the Corps even if everyone else was coming home from the war. The thought of older guys telling sea stories around the neighborhood, and me with none to tell, was more than I could abide. In the spring of 1946, immediately after graduation, I enlisted and left for the Marines' legendary boot camp at Parris Island, South Carolina. Like most teens, I never thought more than a few months ahead; therefore, I never dreamed that 39 years later I would end a career in my beloved Corps as a three-star general.

Hundreds of thousands of youngsters have made the trip to boot camp in the intervening decades. Some spent a few years in the Corps and moved on to other careers. Some were killed or crippled in battle and joined the pantheon of Marine heroes. Some spent their entire adult lives in the Corps, and a few became generals. Regardless of what fate held in store, each of us joined for the same reason—to be a United States Marine. To be a warrior among warriors was the ultimate in machismo, a term we did not use at the time, yet understood. As we prepared for our odyssey, we basked in the reflected glory of the Corps and thrilled to the thought of one day swaggering down the street in a set of dress blues.

But there was that small matter of boot camp first. That rite of passage. That river to cross before the girls would fall all over us on our first leave. For a streetwise kid from the Bronx, Parris Island held no fears. What could be so tough about boot camp?

Reality struck, along with the oppressive summer heat of the Carolina low country, the moment I set foot on Parris Island. Staff Sergeant Petris, a drill instructor from Chester, Pennsylvania, saw to it that my every waking hour would be painfully memorable as I made the passage and crossed that river. It is amazing how all Marines, regardless of generation, remember the name of their drill instructors. Few adults remember their homeroom teacher in high school, but if they served in the Marines, they will remember their DI's name until the day they die. Such is the astounding influence of the sergeants who turn farm boys and city boys alike into basic Marines.

Under the DI's stern tutelage, all of us in Platoon 215 learned that the Marine Corps was more than a fancy uniform. We were constantly reminded by Staff Sergeant Petris, a wounded and decorated survivor of the atoll wars of the Pacific, that we were being trained to fight, survive, and win in the harsh crucible of some unforeseen war. It was a sobering experience.

I remember in the middle of boot camp when a

rumor spread that we would not complete our training, but would be immediately shipped out to China to fight Communists, who were trying to take over that country. I was scared to death and wanted to go home. It was one thing to fantasize in high school about what a gallant and brave Marine I would be, but it was quite another to contemplate the reality of facing death thousands of miles away.

When I look back on that moment of panic, I realize that mine was not an expression of cowardice; it was the normal reaction of a teen-ager who was in the Marine Corps, but not yet a part of it.

Boot camp was just the first step in a process that in time compelled a young man to put the Corps above self. There are legions of young men who experienced the same flash of panic at the prospect of battle and possible death. They overcame their fears over time because their NCOs, non-commissioned officers, and officers molded them into team players who would die before letting their Corps down.

I survived boot camp, and while I didn't get a set of dress blues during those post-war days of fiscal austerity, the forest-green service uniform that I was issued was good enough for me.

Life in the post-war Marine Corps was anticlimactic after the intensity of recruit training. Some of my number did go to China, and some did trade shots with the Chinese communists. My fate was to serve in garrison duty in North Carolina without hearing anything fired outside the rifle range. But my day would come.

In 1947 I was selected for officer training and was sent to Holy Cross College in Massachusetts as part of the first post-war Naval ROTC class. While there, the North Koreans stormed across the 38th parallel to invade their neighbors to the south. When I graduated and was commissioned a second lieutenant in 1951, I knew it would not be long before I would be put to the test, not only as a Marine, but as a leader of Marines.

Officer training at The Basic School in Quantico, Virginia, came immediately on the heels of college and was completed just before Christmas of 1951. I was then certified as a genuine infantry officer and flown out to Korea as a replacement. This time the prospect of battle was real. While there was not the panic I experienced five years earlier as a private, there was, nonetheless, an apprehension of a different kind. Would I measure up? The months of training at Quantico had filled my head with tactics, weapons' characteristics, formulas for demolitions and mortar employment, and the like, but would I remember it all when the time came? Most of all, would I be a good combat leader?

The self-doubts I endured en route to Korea evaporated when I joined the 1st Marines, took command of a rifle platoon, and engaged in my first fire fight five days after leaving the States. I remember the frigid night in the Korean mountains vividly. Star shells, machine-gun tracers, and the flash of artillery explosions reflected against the falling snow like a strobe light in pitch darkness. It was a scene from Dante's *Inferno,* and nothing at all like a John Wayne movie. We did fairly well that night, the first of many similar nights for me.

Few people remember much about the Korean War, but I remember every moment of my part in it. Most of all, I remember the men. My Marines were great, but they were no different from those in the other infantry platoons that made up the 1st Marine Division. I can still name every man who served in my platoon. Corporal Barwick, an automatic rifleman, who doubled as platoon barber, was a standout and a natural fighter. "I love to hear that BAR chat-ter," he would say of his Browning Automatic Rifle. Sergeant Berryman, the platoon guide in charge of supplies, used to ration hand grenades like they were gold, even when we were under attack. "Can't let them waste these things," he would say to me with a conspiratorial wink. Gunnery Sergeant Wagner, my platoon sergeant, watched me carefully in the early days, until he was sure I could be entrusted with his Marines. Wagner was killed on a patrol several months later. I still remember him in my prayers.

The years after Korea and before Vietnam also provided their share of excitement. There was a two-year tour of sea duty aboard the heavy cruiser, U.S.S. *Columbus* (CA-74). Duty with the Navy can be very frustrating for a Marine. The Navy is big on protocol and regulations, but short on things important to Marines, like discipline and spit and polish. I concluded that people who spent two-thirds of their lives at sea standing four-hour watches every eight hours were bound to be a bit weird. For their part, sailors found it strange that Marines liked to wallow in the mud.

In addition to the necessary staff jobs that burden all Marine officers who would rather be in the field, there were other rewarding assignments that honed my professional skills during the late '50s and early '60s. A highlight of those days was a tour with the British Royal Marine commandos. The British taught me a lot about soldiering that stood me in good stead in the following years. I liked the "funny ol' Brits." They dressed differently and talked differently than our Marines, but underneath, a Marine is a Marine the world over. Marines of any nation always get along well, considering troops of other services to be of a lower order. I never met a Soviet Marine, but I suspect we would agree on that point.

In 1959 I rejoined my own Corps as a company commander in the 1st Marine Division at Camp Pendleton, California. It was a high point in my career. The Marine Corps prides itself on being the nation's force in readiness. Then, as now, training takes many forms in various settings. A refrain from the Marines' Hymn sums it up, "In the snow of far-off northern lands/ And in sunny tropic scenes,/ You will find us always on the job,/ The United States Marines." We parachuted into the heat of the Mojave Desert, rappelled down icy mountains in the high Sierras, launched night raids from submarines in the tranquil Pacific, and patrolled through the steaming jungles of Panama. To toughen up, we took summer marches from the floor of Death Valley to the peak of Mount Whitney. New tactics were tested, and new weapons were fired. We trained in helicopter assaults supported by Marine attack aircraft. The Marine specialty of amphibious operations was practiced with the Navy on countless shores. We were ready for anything, and cocky to boot.

In 1965 the call came to put our training to use. The Marines were once again called upon to fight. This time the place was Vietnam.

Oddly enough, I did not serve with Marines during my first tour in that tortured country. My early experience with the Royal Marine commandos and as a reconnaissance officer qualified me to serve as an advisor to a South Vietnamese special operations group. I spent a year with that unit in a shadow war that has yet to be made public. Later, I was to return to Vietnam to command an infantry battalion, and then a reconnaissance unit.

Throughout the war, the Marines fought with the élan that is the hallmark of professionals. We were not unaware of the anti-war demonstrations at home, but that was far away and counted little as we plodded through the rice paddies, alert to the slightest sign of danger.

The Marines I commanded in the Queson Mountains and the An Hoa Basin of Vietnam were no different from their uncles on Hill 749 and along Korea's Imjin River 18 years earlier. They were irreverent, funny, totally self-confident, and deadly. When a young platoon leader, who had cheated death too many times, broke down in tears upon being told to give up his platoon and move to a staff job, I knew how he felt. First loves are memorable. Like all officers, he will always cherish his days in the bush with his first command. His cup would never again be quite as full.

When it was time to leave Vietnam, we marched to the piers and airfields with our heads high, colors flying, and our honor intact. We were glad to be leaving, but not as glad as the North Vietnamese and Vietcong we had battered so badly for six years.

The Marines suffered 103,255 casualties in that war.

Almost 13,000 have their names engraved on a black marble wall in our nation's capital. No one can ever tell a Marine that he lost that war.

With Vietnam a matter of history, Marines did what they always do after a war; they get ready for the next one. A Marine Corps recruiting slogan at the time put it simply and succinctly: "Nobody likes to fight. But somebody has to know how."

After Vietnam, my assignments placed me in positions of greater responsibility in the Corps, and in 1976 I was promoted to brigadier general. My first assignment was the Recruit Depot at Parris Island, where it had all started for me 30 years earlier. I had not been back on the island since the day I happily left with a seabag on my shoulder and two months pay in my pocket.

What a strange sensation to return. I half expected Sergeant Petris to jump from behind a palmetto tree and forcefully remind me which foot was my left. The sights, sounds, and smells were all familiar. As I drove past the drill field, I could hear a chorus of new recruits responding, "YES SIR!" to a DI's rhetorical question. The youngsters on the field seemed terribly young. They stood at awkward attention in brand-new, ill-fitting uniforms. I wondered how those kids could be the heroes of tomorrow's Corps. Yet in a short time the awkwardness would disappear. The chests would fill out and the muscles would bulge to fit the uniform. The look of fright would give way to the glint in the eye that only warriors have, and they would be worthy of the traditions passed on to them. The youngsters I saw on my return to Parris Island are now senior NCOs.

They have fought in Lebanon and Grenada, and today serve in the Persian Gulf, adding their own chapter to Marine Corps history—a legacy for new Marines.

After two years at Parris Island, I went to Quantico in 1978 as director of professional education and, eventually, to Marine Corps Headquarters. There I was involved in the plans, policies, and operations of the Corps. The Corps was in the best shape of my career. The individual Marine was smarter and tougher than when I entered the Corps. New equipment and weapons rolled in as part of a Corps-wide modernization program. The infantry had a new light-armored vehicle to give it tactical mobility on the battlefield. A hybrid helicopter-airplane called the Osprey was being developed to carry troops, replacing the war-weary CH-46 helicopters of the Vietnam era. More powerful artillery and tanks were being fielded, along with improved anti-tank weapons and individual small arms. Equipment to support three airlifted brigades was being pre-positioned in ships strategically located at sea near the world's trouble spots. The Fleet Marine Force was improving its counter-terrorism capabilities by undertaking vigorous training in special operations and raiding.

It was a great time to be a Marine, but for this general, it was time to leave the business of soldiering to a younger breed of warrior. The Corps was in good shape and in good hands. It was the perfect time to make my final muster.

On a beautiful June day in 1985, I stood at attention for my retirement parade at the Marine Barracks in Washington, D.C. While the band marched past playing the Marines' Hymn, I reflected on my years in the Corps. I also smiled at the thought that somewhere in America, there was a teen-ager like myself, almost four decades earlier, on his way to boot camp. He already pictured himself swaggering down the street in dress blues with a girl on each arm. But my picture of him was different. He was my replacement, and some 40 years hence would also stand where I was standing for his last parade. I silently wished him luck, whoever he was, and hoped he would have as much fun getting here as I did.

—Bernard E. Trainor

(Overleaf, pages 20-21) The wheatfield at Belleau Wood, France, where over 400 Marines became casualties on June 6, 1918. This photograph was taken at 0600, the time of the attack, exactly 67 years later.

Machine-gun positions providing interlocking fire were mapped out
on the kitchen table of a nearby farmhouse by a Marine lieutenant
at the Battle of Belleau Wood, France.

BELLEAU WOOD

At first glance, the village of Belleau looks like a thousand other sleepy country towns in the Champagne region of France. The town square includes a goldfish pond, a pale-yellow mailbox, a modern phone booth, and a small bakery that doubles as social center and general store. The houses are solid old farm buildings, built by earlier generations with the heavy, gray stones of the region. Occasionally, a car passes through town. Women in black head scarves stop and chat as they go about their shopping.

The mayor's office in the village of Belleau proudly displays the U.S. Marine Corps colors. People smile radiantly if they spot a Marine Corps bumper sticker. "Ah, *les marines*," they say, "*nos amis,* our friends."

In May 1918, Germany's armies embarked on their last major offensive of World War I. Superbly led and disciplined, the German troops poured through an opening in French defenses and advanced to within 56 miles of Paris. Panic ensued. Parisians piled their belongings into carts and fled. French troops fell back in disorder. Senior Allied generals and important French political figures considered asking for an immediate armistice. The French government prepared for flight.

To delay the rapid German advance, the Allied high command ordered the American 2nd Division to make a stand. The 2nd Division included the 4th Marine Brigade, consisting of the 5th and 6th Marine Regiments and the 6th Machine-gun Battalion. Most of the men had just arrived in France, after only eight weeks of training at Parris Island, South Carolina. They had barely been tested in battle.

The Marines moved up to the front. "They looked fine, coming in there, tall fellows, healthy and fit," a U.S. Army officer later wrote, "and we all felt better. We knew something was going to happen." As the Marines passed disoriented and demoralized French troops, a high-ranking French officer urged them to retreat back to safety.

"Retreat? Hell, we just got here," Captain Lloyd Williams is said to have replied.

The 2nd Division held a front 11 miles long. The Marine regiments, just north of the Paris-Metz highway, faced the crack Prussian 461st Infantry Regiment. On June 2, 1918, the Germans again advanced, then dug in at a wooded area known as the Bois de Belleau, a game preserve once used by the kings of France.

On June 6, the Marines faced a wide, rolling wheatfield that led up to a hilly area of woodlands. Entrenched in the forest were 1,200 German troops. The wheat in the field offered the only cover from devastating German machine-gun fire.

Three times the Marines charged the German position. Three times they fell back. During what was recorded as the hottest day of the year, the Marines shed their blouses and attacked bare-chested. Water ran short. Casualties were heavy. Only after the fourth charge did they succeed in gaining a toehold in the woods.

Official military reports of the battle record the amazement of German officers at the marksmanship of the Marines. The Springfield '03 rifle was supposed to be accurate for a distance of 450 yards. Yet the Marines were causing casualties at the incredible distance of 800 yards.

"I am up front and entering Belleau Wood with

the U.S. Marines," *Chicago Tribune* reporter Floyd Gibbons wrote on the evening of June 6. "The oats and wheat in the open field were waving and snapping off —not from the wind but from the rifle and machine-gun fire of German veterans in their well-concealed positions. The sergeant swung his bayoneted rifle over his head with a forward sweep. He yelled at his men, 'Come on, you sons-of-bitches. Do you want to live forever?'"

The casualties were massive. The Marines lost 1,087 men killed and wounded that day, close to 20 percent of brigade strength.

The battle raged for another 20 days. Then, on June 26, 1918, Major Maurice Shearer, commanding officer of the 3rd Battalion, 5th Marines, sent his famous message: "Woods now U.S. Marine Corps' entirely." Belleau Wood had at last been cleared of German troops. To honor the Marines, General Degoutte, commanding the French 6th Army, on June 30 decreed, "Henceforth in all official papers, Belleau Wood shall bear the name, 'Bois de la Brigade de Marine.'"

The mayor of Belleau raises Charolais cattle, a highly prized breed in France. In June 1981, one of his cows stepped on a live 75mm artillery shell. The cow died. The mayor, an experienced farmer, is stoic about the loss. He lives in an old farmhouse in the center of town, which still bears traces of machine-gun fire and shrapnel on its walls.

"I hope," he said some time ago, "that Marines will always find a warm welcome in Belleau, that our little village will be for them a little bit of their own place, for they came to this country when it was in danger. I think I know my fellow villagers well enough

to say that they share this hope with me, particularly the older ones."

One of the "older ones" lives alone atop a low hill near Belleau with his three dogs, his lovingly polished hunting rifles, and his memories. He was six years old when the Marines occupied his father's farmhouse on June 5, 1918. The building still stands, although a portion of it is in ruins, destroyed by German artillery fire. He remembers the sounds of battle, the wounded, the dead. He remembers a young Marine lieutenant who would later become a general. The lieutenant drew detailed maps in order to deploy machine-gun positions. The old man proudly displays the lieutenant's map, and the shallow pits scattered about the farm, to visitors.

Marines assigned to guard the U.S. Embassy in Paris are frequent visitors to Belleau. They come for Memorial Day parades, to spend weekends with the local Boy Scouts, and one Marine was recently married in the village church. Others simply drive out to be alone at the battlefield.

"I just get lost, spellbound when I come here," says one Marine. "I think about what it would be like to have fought here. In boot camp you have classes about the history of the Corps. They tell you about the fierce fighting at Belleau Wood and you take pride in the tradition.

"As a Marine, a part of my history is here. Marines fought and died here. I get all rattled by it. I walk through the fields into the woods and out to the perimeter where the Germans had their machine-gun nests. This is my history."

Some years ago, several young Marine lieutenants

They have fought in Lebanon and Grenada, and today serve in the Persian Gulf, adding their own chapter to Marine Corps history—a legacy for new Marines.

After two years at Parris Island, I went to Quantico in 1978 as director of professional education and, eventually, to Marine Corps Headquarters. There I was involved in the plans, policies, and operations of the Corps. The Corps was in the best shape of my career. The individual Marine was smarter and tougher than when I entered the Corps. New equipment and weapons rolled in as part of a Corps-wide modernization program. The infantry had a new light-armored vehicle to give it tactical mobility on the battlefield. A hybrid helicopter-airplane called the Osprey was being developed to carry troops, replacing the war-weary CH-46 helicopters of the Vietnam era. More powerful artillery and tanks were being fielded, along with improved anti-tank weapons and individual small arms. Equipment to support three airlifted brigades was being pre-positioned in ships strategically located at sea near the world's trouble spots. The Fleet Marine Force was improving its counter-terrorism capabilities by undertaking vigorous training in special operations and raiding.

It was a great time to be a Marine, but for this general, it was time to leave the business of soldiering to a younger breed of warrior. The Corps was in good shape and in good hands. It was the perfect time to make my final muster.

On a beautiful June day in 1985, I stood at attention for my retirement parade at the Marine Barracks in Washington, D.C. While the band marched past playing the Marines' Hymn, I reflected on my years in the Corps. I also smiled at the thought that somewhere in America, there was a teen-ager like myself, almost four decades earlier, on his way to boot camp. He already pictured himself swaggering down the street in dress blues with a girl on each arm. But my picture of him was different. He was my replacement, and some 40 years hence would also stand where I was standing for his last parade. I silently wished him luck, whoever he was, and hoped he would have as much fun getting here as I did.

—Bernard E. Trainor

(Overleaf, pages 20-21) The wheatfield at Belleau Wood, France, where over 400 Marines became casualties on June 6, 1918. This photograph was taken at 0600, the time of the attack, exactly 67 years later.

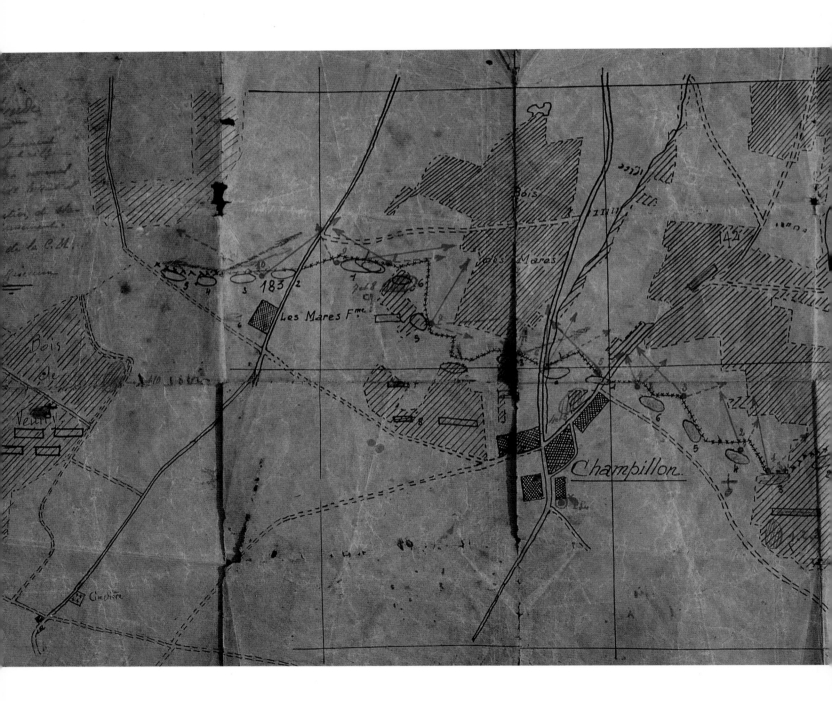

Machine-gun positions providing interlocking fire were mapped out on the kitchen table of a nearby farmhouse by a Marine lieutenant at the Battle of Belleau Wood, France.

BELLEAU WOOD

At first glance, the village of Belleau looks like a thousand other sleepy country towns in the Champagne region of France. The town square includes a goldfish pond, a pale-yellow mailbox, a modern phone booth, and a small bakery that doubles as social center and general store. The houses are solid old farm buildings, built by earlier generations with the heavy, gray stones of the region. Occasionally, a car passes through town. Women in black head scarves stop and chat as they go about their shopping.

The mayor's office in the village of Belleau proudly displays the U.S. Marine Corps colors. People smile radiantly if they spot a Marine Corps bumper sticker. "Ah, *les marines*," they say, "*nos amis,* our friends."

In May 1918, Germany's armies embarked on their last major offensive of World War I. Superbly led and disciplined, the German troops poured through an opening in French defenses and advanced to within 56 miles of Paris. Panic ensued. Parisians piled their belongings into carts and fled. French troops fell back in disorder. Senior Allied generals and important French political figures considered asking for an immediate armistice. The French government prepared for flight.

To delay the rapid German advance, the Allied high command ordered the American 2nd Division to make a stand. The 2nd Division included the 4th Marine Brigade, consisting of the 5th and 6th Marine Regiments and the 6th Machine-gun Battalion. Most of the men had just arrived in France, after only eight weeks of training at Parris Island, South Carolina. They had barely been tested in battle.

The Marines moved up to the front. "They looked fine, coming in there, tall fellows, healthy and fit," a U.S. Army officer later wrote, "and we all felt better. We knew something was going to happen." As the Marines passed disoriented and demoralized French troops, a high-ranking French officer urged them to retreat back to safety.

"Retreat? Hell, we just got here," Captain Lloyd Williams is said to have replied.

The 2nd Division held a front 11 miles long. The Marine regiments, just north of the Paris-Metz highway, faced the crack Prussian 461st Infantry Regiment. On June 2, 1918, the Germans again advanced, then dug in at a wooded area known as the Bois de Belleau, a game preserve once used by the kings of France.

On June 6, the Marines faced a wide, rolling wheatfield that led up to a hilly area of woodlands. Entrenched in the forest were 1,200 German troops. The wheat in the field offered the only cover from devastating German machine-gun fire.

Three times the Marines charged the German position. Three times they fell back. During what was recorded as the hottest day of the year, the Marines shed their blouses and attacked bare-chested. Water ran short. Casualties were heavy. Only after the fourth charge did they succeed in gaining a toehold in the woods.

Official military reports of the battle record the amazement of German officers at the marksmanship of the Marines. The Springfield '03 rifle was supposed to be accurate for a distance of 450 yards. Yet the Marines were causing casualties at the incredible distance of 800 yards.

"I am up front and entering Belleau Wood with

the U.S. Marines," *Chicago Tribune* reporter Floyd Gibbons wrote on the evening of June 6. "The oats and wheat in the open field were waving and snapping off —not from the wind but from the rifle and machine-gun fire of German veterans in their well-concealed positions. The sergeant swung his bayoneted rifle over his head with a forward sweep. He yelled at his men, 'Come on, you sons-of-bitches. Do you want to live forever?'"

The casualties were massive. The Marines lost 1,087 men killed and wounded that day, close to 20 percent of brigade strength.

The battle raged for another 20 days. Then, on June 26, 1918, Major Maurice Shearer, commanding officer of the 3rd Battalion, 5th Marines, sent his famous message: "Woods now U.S. Marine Corps' entirely." Belleau Wood had at last been cleared of German troops. To honor the Marines, General Degoutte, commanding the French 6th Army, on June 30 decreed, "Hence forth in all official papers, Belleau Wood shall bear the name, 'Bois de la Brigade de Marine.'"

The mayor of Belleau raises Charolais cattle, a highly prized breed in France. In June 1981, one of his cows stepped on a live 75mm artillery shell. The cow died. The mayor, an experienced farmer, is stoic about the loss. He lives in an old farmhouse in the center of town, which still bears traces of machine-gun fire and shrapnel on its walls.

"I hope," he said some time ago, "that Marines will always find a warm welcome in Belleau, that our little village will be for them a little bit of their own place, for they came to this country when it was in danger. I think I know my fellow villagers well enough to say that they share this hope with me, particularly the older ones."

One of the "older ones" lives alone atop a low hill near Belleau with his three dogs, his lovingly polished hunting rifles, and his memories. He was six years old when the Marines occupied his father's farmhouse on June 5, 1918. The building still stands, although a portion of it is in ruins, destroyed by German artillery fire. He remembers the sounds of battle, the wounded, the dead. He remembers a young Marine lieutenant who would later become a general. The lieutenant drew detailed maps in order to deploy machine-gun positions. The old man proudly displays the lieutenant's map, and the shallow pits scattered about the farm, to visitors.

Marines assigned to guard the U.S. Embassy in Paris are frequent visitors to Belleau. They come for Memorial Day parades, to spend weekends with the local Boy Scouts, and one Marine was recently married in the village church. Others simply drive out to be alone at the battlefield.

"I just get lost, spellbound when I come here," says one Marine. "I think about what it would be like to have fought here. In boot camp you have classes about the history of the Corps. They tell you about the fierce fighting at Belleau Wood and you take pride in the tradition.

"As a Marine, a part of my history is here. Marines fought and died here. I get all rattled by it. I walk through the fields into the woods and out to the perimeter where the Germans had their machine-gun nests. This is my history."

Some years ago, several young Marine lieutenants

Some 2,288 Marines, soldiers, and sailors are buried in the wheatfields of Belleau, France, just 400 yards from the German cemetery.

were on liberty in France and visited Belleau. "They were quite well behaved," recalls a man who for more than 12 years has maintained the Belleau cemetery. "They walked around and looked at things. The wheat was tall and nearly ready for harvest in the field where so many Marines died that one day.

"Those lieutenants lost all their composure. One started and the others followed. In full uniform, they charged across the field, yelling and screaming, falling down and crawling as if they were under fire, scrambling up again, and charging the silent woods. It was quite a scene.

"The farmer was upset when he saw his field the next day. But when he learned it was Marines who had trampled the wheat, he was actually pleased."

Each May Belleau celebrates American Memorial Day. Marines come from Paris and parade through the village. There is a little ceremony, some speeches, music, and a detachment of French Marines. After the formalities, the people assemble in the courtyard of the old castle of Belleau and drink champagne.

"If you are a U.S. Marine," says an embassy guard who has come for the event, "they treat you like a king." For hours the French and Americans toast each other, in memory of the desperate battle.

Many traces of the struggle remain. In the village's small church, rebuilt by Americans after World War I, is a stained-glass window depicting a U.S. Marine with a French *poilu*. There is a plaque that reads, "For the children of Belleau who died 1914-1918." An old teacher still relates stories of the nightmares that awakened children in the village long after the war was over.

In the village cemetery is a simple grave. The man who is buried there was a Marine who came back to

Belleau after the war to see the graves of his friends. One night he committed suicide. "He wanted to be with them," explains an old man. The villagers bought a plot and buried him, and maintain his grave to this day. "He had no family," says the old man.

The military cemetery at the edge of the woods is a serene place. Forsythia, laurel, boxwood, Japanese plum, deutzie, mock orange, Oregon grape, and beds of polyantha roses surround the graves. Two thousand two hundred and eighty-eight Americans are buried here. Among them are the graves of 249 unknowns. During World War II, the Germans who occupied France left the American colors flying at the cemetery, even after the United States had entered the war. Some 350 yards away is the German cemetery, which, like the American cemetery, borders the fatal wheatfield.

Marines like to be called "Devil Dogs," a nickname given them by the Germans at Belleau. When German troops first occupied the village at the beginning of the war, they broke into the courtyard of the castle of Belleau. Ferocious bull mastiffs, a breed of powerful, smooth-coated animals used since the days of the Roman Caesars as war dogs, attacked the Germans. Weighing more than 180 pounds, these "Hounds of Belleau" had served as guard dogs at the castle for centuries. The German troops referred to these massive creatures as *Teufelshunde,* or "Devil Dogs." Evidently the fierce assaults of the American Marines reminded the Germans of the bull mastiffs they had encountered at the castle, and the name stuck.

Today, in the ruins of the castle is a life-size bronze likeness of the head of a bull mastiff, a fountain for ice-cold water. It is said that Marines slaked their thirst at this spot during the Battle of Belleau. Over the years, the true source of the nickname has given way to a comparatively gentle English bulldog mascot that carries on the tradition of the Devil Dogs, the fierce Hounds of Belleau.

The bulldog is not the only trace of Belleau in the Marine Corps today. After the battle, France awarded the 5th and 6th Marines with the fourragere in the colors of the ribbon of the Croix de Guerre. This decoration, roughly equivalent to the Presidential Unit Citation, is still worn by the two regiments.

Franklin Delano Roosevelt, assistant secretary of the Navy during World War I, left another mark. Inspecting the Marines in August 1918, he directed that enlisted Marines be allowed to wear the Corps emblem on their collars, as did their officers.

Of greater significance is the tactical influence of the battle. Rifle squads and fire teams, the smallest organized units in combat, remain to this day the keystone of Marine Corps infantry tactics. On June 6, 1918, the Marine units did as they had been taught. They attacked in close formation, running up against heavy German machine-gun fire. Three times they charged, and were repulsed. As casualties mounted, the Marines anticipated present-day Corps doctrine, and split into small teams. While one team charged, another provided cover with rifle and machine-gun fire.

"The Marines went back to Indian warfare," a Marine officer who studied the battle says. "They did not play by the rules of the First World War, which dictated that when you meet resistance, you dig trenches. The Marines did not dig trenches. They used trees and rocks for cover and attacked in small groups. It worked."

In the woods, close to the sign with the official name "Bois de la Brigade de Marine," is a black granite and steel monument. A life-size bronze bas-relief by Felix de Weldon depicts a bare-chested Marine attacking with rifle and fixed bayonet.

Traces of the conflict may be found everywhere in the woods of Belleau. There are 11 tons of metal in each acre of the battleground. No structures can be built here. Unexploded shells containing high explosives or mustard gas contaminate the fields and forest loam. Each spring more of these shells work their way to the surface. Walking about, I find old helmets, canteens, wooden spikes, USMC bread boxes, the barrel of a Springfield '03 rifle. Once in a while, human remains will be found. A skull, still wearing a German helmet, was discovered in a treetop. Five complete Marine Corps first-aid kits were also found in a tree, placed there perhaps in the heat of battle, then forgotten.

The trees tell the story. Some have been so mutilated by shrapnel that it is difficult to imagine how they survived. I dig into the bark of a trunk, and turn out some rusty fragments. Perhaps some young Marine took shelter here, or perhaps a young German soldier. The wind stirs slightly in the leaves. When the last survivor of the battle is dead, the trees will still brandish the scars of the withering fire where thousands of men died.

Marine Corps Barracks mascot "Lance Corporal Chesty VI" earns his pay as a somewhat unruly participant at parades. He bears little resemblance to the famed "Devil Dogs" of Belleau Wood, France, fierce bull mastiffs that German troops encountered at a castle near the battle scene.

Drill seems endless on the sultry tarmac at Parris Island, South Carolina.

BORN ON PARRIS ISLAND

I was born one summer day,
One winter night
On Parris Island, South Carolina.
Where the sun is mighty hot
Where's the land that God forgot
Where's the sand that's mighty deep
Oh yea…
Parris Island, South Carolina
Oh yea…
Makes you lean
Makes you mean
Oh yea…
The green machine
Fightin' machine
Here we are
Runnin' hard
Workin' hard
Trainin' hard
Oh yea…

— Marine Corps Cadence

"That you have chosen the United States Marine Corps as the service in which you wish to serve sets you apart," an officer addresses a group of "boots," young recruits, at Parris Island, South Carolina. "It is proof of the fact that you want a challenge. It will not be easy. You're going to find the training tough. I demand that you put forth your maximum effort 100 percent of the time. Nothing less will be tolerated. For the next 11 weeks, we're going to test your ability and your desire to earn the title of Marine. In doing so, I promise each one of you your fair chance to prove your worth to the Marine Corps."

Arriving in the middle of the night, recruits have been herded, inspected, and yelled at. With heads shorn like sheep, overwhelmed by a whole new military world, they wait in line to be issued strange equipment. Many feel abandoned, lost forever beyond the steaming swamps that separate subtropical Parris Island from the mainland.

What kind of individual comes here? "We've had quite a cross section, ranging from a momma's boy to the hood who's got a record as long as your arm," explains a receiving sergeant.

But recruits bring no personal history to boot camp. Worth is measured not by education or social background, but by will. "Marines are born on Parris Island," says a colonel in charge of the Recruit Training Regiment.

"It's important that right now you begin developing the one trait that has separated the United States Marine Corps from all other services," a drill instructor barks at a silent group of 74 nervous youngsters, sitting on the polished concrete of their squad bay. "You must never give up, you must never quit. Make no mistake — it won't be easy. We will help you, we will teach you, but we cannot do it for you. There's only one way for you to become a Marine. You must prove to us that you should have the right to share the title and the prestige of being a United States Marine."

A colonel addresses the raw recruits on the subject of their drill instructors. "They know exactly what to do with you. They know exactly what it takes to distress you a little bit, by another word, what makes you tick. They are interested in seeing how many of you are good enough to be United States Marines. Not all of you will be able to make it.

"But these DIs will never give up on you. As long as they think you're trying and as long as they think that you want to be a Marine, they'll hang in there with you. But the moment you give up on yourself, the moment you quit on yourself, they will be finished with you."

Never give up. Never surrender. The DI will spare no effort to instill that spirit in his "maggots," the recruits whom he alternately rebukes, cajoles, and derides, and whom he loves. They are his charges, his "kids." He will do everything in his power to prepare them "to go in the line and do their bit for the Corps."

A drill instructor shakes his head and smiles the sad smile that comes from having seen too many young men die. He has 28 years in the Marine Corps and three tours of duty in Vietnam.

"Mothers of America say, 'Take my Johnny, make a man out of him, but don't hurt his feelings.' Well, I'll hurt his feelings if I can keep him alive at a later date. I'd much rather hurt his feelings here than have him lose an arm or a leg or his life," he says. "If I never have to zip another kid into a body bag, it will be too soon."

Forty thousand enlisted Marines are trained each year at two recruit depots — Parris Island and San Diego, California. The depots are equally tough, equally demanding. But Parris Island is the legend.

When World War I started, Parris Island had only been in operation for a few months. "During the day we trained," recalls a Marine veteran of WWI, "At night we built the roads." The Marine Corps allowed just eight weeks of basic training at Parris Island and two or three weeks of combat training at Quantico, Virginia, before shipping troops to France. Recruits in the other services usually went through six months of training. "France was a sinecure after Parris Island," says the veteran. "We didn't care that we were going to war. All we cared about was getting away from Parris Island."

Graduates of Parris Island might refer to their counterparts from San Diego as "Lace Pants Marines" or "Hollywood Marines," but the differences lie in geography only. The graduates are virtually indistinguishable.

Boot camp is traumatic. The door is closed on the

rest of the world. All personal belongings, with a few rare exceptions, are taken away and stored. For nearly three months, the recruit is allowed no contact with anyone outside his platoon.

"The isolation is complete and probably exceeds that of many prisons," says a Marine officer. "Recruits are deliberately made to feel fumbling, inept, helpless, and outraged."

A drill instructor explains the process. "We tear 'em down to build 'em up again as Marines," he says. "We make 'em growl and scream, we make 'em feel bad, we make 'em feel mad, we reduce them to the lowest common denominator."

The recruits are forced to search inside themselves for a restorative. "The cure is pride," says a Marine officer. "After getting torn apart, they get fighting spirit, get proud. It cures, it heals, it makes Marines. It makes Marines who will go fight for their buddies, for their Corps."

The training at Parris Island and San Diego sticks. "Boot camp marks you for life," says a retired commandant. "My drill instructor lit a fire in me 40 years ago. It's still burning and will until I die.

"You take an individual and give him or her more to do, more challenges than he could ever imagine," the retired commandant continues, "and if he does it, and does it well, it builds confidence. Two things are emphasized constantly: spirit and discipline. That training prepares the recruits for the ideals of sacrifice and honor."

The commandant recalls asking a graduating private the meaning of discipline. "Sir, the private will always do whatever needs to be done, no matter what, sir," was the response.

The elements of Marine Corps boot camp are relatively commonplace: running, push-ups, rifle training, forced marches, bayonet drill, pugil sticks, heat, sand fleas, basic infantry tactics, spit shining boots. And endless drill.

The long, hot parade deck turns torrid even on winter days. Drill. Running. Drill. Screaming. Discipline. Motivation. Pride. Life is reduced to only a few words. "My Corps." "Your Corps." "Our Corps." Ceaseless is the incantation of the names of famous Marine Corps battles like Belleau Wood, Chateau Thierry, Iwo Jima, Inchon, Guadalcanal, Chosin, Khe Sanh.

"When they graduate they will be unable to even think of letting down their buddies, their Corps, their family," says a drill instructor.

Training is hard and counts. But what Marines value the most, what stays with them for life, is the unique spirit and camaraderie of belonging to a special band of brothers.

"Sir, the recruit joined the Marine Corps because he feels it's the finest fighting force in the world today, sir, and also, sir, the recruit wants to learn how to defend his country and his fellow Marines," says a three-week-old recruit.

Age is measured by days in boot camp; over a period of 11 weeks, the recruits grow up, evolving in the lexicon of their drill instructors from "You maggots," to "You people," to "Privates," and, after final inspection and graduation, to "Marines." While young men and women must face their personal limitations at boot camp, they take satisfaction in knowing that they have proven their mettle as acolytes of an elite fighting force.

When older Marines think of boot camp, when memories take on a cadence and pass in review, they will speak with respect about their drill instructors, of the deep emotional scars the tear-down-build-up process of Parris Island and San Diego left, and of their immense pride in being numbered among "America's Best."

Each individual was "measured with the same simple yardstick: Was a man dependable and honest, or would he cut and run and steal you blind," wrote one Marine decades after boot camp. "Years later, as I watched some young men pirate ideas from one another or duck under a desk when trouble was at hand, I remembered the Island."

(Above) Parris Island, South Carolina. (Overleaf, pages 32-33) Drill instructor, Parris Island.

The barracks at Parris Island, South Carolina, built in World War II, are freezing in winter, steaming in summer. The island lies just below sea level, and all its steam pipes and water lines run above ground.

Forming ranks, Parris Island.

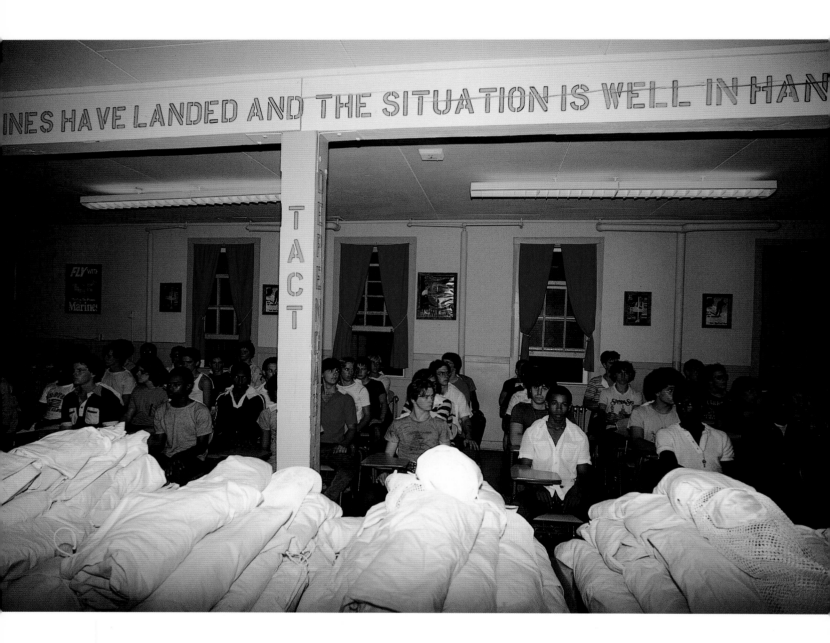

"There is nothing so scary as your first night on the Island," a receiving sergeant at Parris Island, South Carolina, comments.

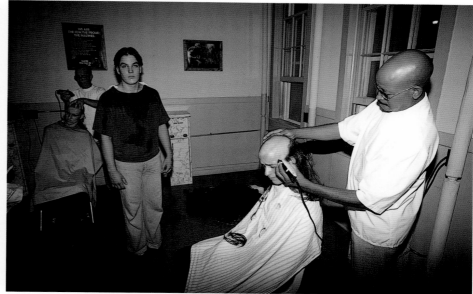

The 15-second haircut and simultaneous dental X-rays provide recruits with a strong dose of military efficiency.

Platoon 3040 is one of thousands, but the number will be unforgettable to the men and women who followed that guidon through 11
wrenching weeks of boot camp.

"It was good for Chesty Puller; It is good enough for me. It was good at Wake Island; It is good enough for me. It was good at Guadalcanal; It is good enough for me. It was good in Vietnam...," is a cadence at Parris Island, South Carolina. Marine Corps history is constantly affirmed in the minds of recruits.

"The platoon that can master close-order drill is the platoon that has
learned to work as a team, and that's what the Corps is all about!"
shouts a drill instructor on Parris Island, South Carolina.

Women Marines receive basic rifle training and other combat skills. Although excluded from serving in combat billets by an act of Congress, women are trained for defensive combat. In "tomorrow's war the rear can become the front real quick," a sergeant comments.

(Above and facing) Teamwork and challenge make the Marine.

(Overleaf, pages 44-45) "Gimme some of that good Marine Corps spirit!" Platoon members cheer as two combatants engage in pugil sticks training.

(Above and facing) The "Slide for Life" is easier than it looks and builds confidence, although many recruits get their spirits dampened in the process.

(Above and facing) Sweat and fear are the cheapest commodities on Parris Island, South Carolina. (Overleaf, pages 50-51) "If you want to be a Marine, you have to learn to love mud. Mud is your friend. Mud is your cover. Mud is good for you," exhorts a drill instructor at Parris Island.

Frugality is a Marine Corps trait. Brass is collected and sold for scrap.

A recruit throws a grenade. "It's you and your buddy. When the chips are down, that's what counts. The bond between you and your fellow Marine."

(Above and facing) "To earn the title of Marine is your greatest accomplishment here. Nobody can take that away from you," a speaker addresses the graduates on Parris Island, South Carolina.

GRUNTS

Some are tall, some are short, some look as powerful as bulldozers, others remind you of the kid in high school who was always the last one picked when sides were chosen for a game. They come from all over the United States. They are "grunts"—U.S. Marine Corps riflemen.

Some will claim that a Marine rifleman is the most lethal and reliable weapon ever invented. Every Marine —pilot, aircraft mechanic, cook, baker, infantryman, artilleryman, tank commander, or computer programmer —is a rifleman first. He or she will requalify with the weapon once a year. Marines don't wear patches, unit insignia, or badges. A Marine Corps aviator's uniform, of course, includes the wings of a pilot, but many Marine pilots will respond, when asked about their occupation, "I'm a Marine rifleman, temporarily assigned to flight duty."

Some Marines are permanently assigned the role of rifleman, serving in any of the Corps' 27 infantry battalions. Their Military Occupational Specialty (MOS) is '03. They are grunts. The Marines who served in Beirut, Lebanon, were grunts, for the most part. The Marines who assaulted the beaches at Tarawa and Guadalcanal were grunts. Films like *The Sands of Iwo Jima* have etched the Marine Corps infantryman indelibly into the American mind.

For grunts in the field, life offers no creature comforts. It may be humid, buggy, rainy, windy, dusty, brutally cold, or so hot that the sun blisters the skin. Whatever the climate, the weather is almost certain to be extreme. Grunts must carry a heavy pack, assorted weapons and ammunition, and enough food and water to subsist for at least a couple of days. Sometimes the grunts get lost, and accurate information is hard to come by. When they aren't riding in a claustrophobic, uncomfortable contraption called an amtrac, they must tramp through mud, snow, or rocky terrain.

Life for a grunt is miserable, yet most Marines relish it. A good many men join the Corps for MOS '03 —infantry, but you would never suspect it after listening to Marines in the field.

Grunts grumble, curse, growl, complain, groan, moan, grouse, and lament all day and all night. They refer to this as "bitching." Nothing is ever right. From the Commandant of the Corps on down, everybody is in conspiracy against them. If it rains, it's the fault of some general who wants to make life miserable. If combat rations have disappeared from the supply line, it's evidence of a conspiracy. Most catastrophes are caused by the "higher command," a mysterious, faceless organization that is totally ignorant of the grunts' needs in the field and on which the onus for nearly every misfortune is placed.

On a train pulling out from Howard Air Force Base in Panama's Canal Zone, a battalion of Marines talks, plays practical jokes, and bitches. They bitch about the inadequacies of the KC-135 transport aircraft and the slow train. They bitch about the lousy rations. They bitch about the heat. They bitch about the disorganization of the troop movement.

The grunts are heading 53 miles across Panama, through dense jungles, to Ft. Sherman, location of the Jungle Warfare School. As the train plunges deeper and deeper into the jungle, large tree branches whip the

(Facing) Masked with camouflage paint, a warrior mentally prepares himself for an exercise.

metal roofs of the cars. The Marines are quiet.

"They realize they have to hump through that," says a gunnery sergeant, explaining the unusual silence. "If they don't bitch," he continues, "they ain't happy. I get real worried when I hear no bitching."

Grunts will relate harrowing tales about life in the field. Based on fact, though embellished with particularly impressive details, the stories confirm the difficulties of life in the field. The motive is straightforward enough; making the job sound painful or demanding will earn an extra measure of respect for its execution. But these stories have another, more subtle aim; grunts don't want "higher headquarters" or the general population to realize that they actually enjoy covering their faces with camouflage paint, sleeping in muddy ditches, and humping around a desert carrying a heavy pack.

"Many of these guys joined the Corps to do exactly this kind of stuff," says a lieutenant colonel and battalion commander. "It's all that adventure training—rappelling down cliffs, crossing rivers, jumping out of helicopters."

Even the leaders like it. "Being a Marine officer is the only job where you can be doing deadly serious work and play like a little kid at the same time," says a Marine infantry officer.

The history of warfare over the past 3,000 years indicates that creature comforts have little to do with high morale in a fighting unit or the ability to win. Under good leadership, an infantryman will accept the hardships of life in the field, including the most savage combat, where casualties lie right and left and the primary motivation might be fear.

"The life expectancy of a lieutenant in combat is about two minutes," a second lieutenant explains. His voice betrays no emotion.

During operations in the Mojave Desert, infantry and tank units are preparing for an exercise that the Marines refer to as "Final Protective Fire." It is late at night, and tanks, infantry, artillery, and anti-tank gunners are lined up across a valley in the Bullion Mountains. Upon orders, they open fire, attempting to destroy an advancing "enemy." Live ammunition is used. It is like watching the end of the world. Tracer rounds spew forth from machine guns and tanks, and rockets zig-zag across the desert floor, bounding off rocks and exploding a mile or two away. A river of hot, flying lead pours from the line. "It's kind of funny to think," says one lieutenant watching the exercise, "that we'll die one day running around in something like this."

There is little talk about dying. Talking about death in combat situations is a jinx, like pilots talking about crashes. They discuss "casualties." Yet all the grunts think about death. They think about it during combat exercises when the umpire declares them dead; they must wait four hours to come back to life, more than sufficient time to think about being dead.

Reminders of the implications of war are subtle —the chaplain, the corpsmen, the two dog tags around your neck, one to be collected, and one to stay with your body.

"Civilians cannot and never will understand the psychology which causes the Marine Corps fighting man to kill with the one hand," a Marine writes in a recent book, "and caress with the other." The contrast can be a shock.

I watch a snarling, weathered gunnery sergeant, who never has a kind word to say and is reputed to have smiled only once in his 33 years on earth, holding the hand of a young Marine who has broken his leg jumping from a helicopter skid. Talking quietly to the Marine, he helps the corpsman with the field dressing. Periodically, the "gunny" threatens some distant radio operator and flight dispatcher with unmentionable acts for being slow in providing a helicopter for evacuation of the injured Marine.

Grunts can and will be hard on each other, not accepting insubordination, sloppiness, or laziness, but from boot camp on, they learn and practice the old saying, "Marines take care of their own." They learn, in a hard and tested way, how to stand and fight when all their instincts tell them to run. They hear over and over that they will take care of other Marines; they will do so in combat, in their personal lives, and in their civilian occupations.

Grunts will not leave wounded or dead behind. Unforgettable are pictures from the Korean War, where Marines had to fight their way to the coast after running into several Chinese divisions at the Chosin Reservoir. The wounded and the dead were stacked like firewood on jeeps, trucks, and tanks. "There is some comfort in knowing that you won't be left out there," a Marine says.

Many military writers have noted that an individual in battle fights primarily for his friends. He doesn't want them to suffer; he doesn't want to let them down. Frequently grunts have stayed behind to cover the retreat of their unit, facing certain death.

Nowhere is it written that a Marine should jump on a hand grenade to protect another Marine, but stories of grunts who have done so are always told in boot camp. "The kids have so much history drummed into their brains," says one Marine captain, "that they will do anything to avoid letting Marine Corps tradition down."

For the grunts, taking care of each other is a strong, lasting bond.

(Overleaf, pages 60-61) Jungle Warfare Training, Ft. Sherman, Panama. The Marine Corps developed the technique of "vertical envelopment," skillful use of helicopters to insert combat troops near enemy positions quickly.

(Facing) Grunts from the 3rd Battalion, 2nd Marines, on a "Mike boat," Rio Chagres, Panama. (Above) Ft. Sherman, Panama.

(Above) Jungle Warfare Training, Ft. Sherman, Panama. (Facing)
"There are no shortcuts for the Marine rifleman," says an officer.
"With all the high-tech gear, and all the air support, and all the artil-
lery, it is still the Marine grunt who has to close with the enemy."

SIZE UP THE SITUATION

UNDUE HASTE MAKES WASTE

REMEMBER WHERE YOU ARE

VANQUISH FEAR AND PANIC

IMPROVISE

VALUE LIVING

ACT LIKE THE NATIVES

LEARN BASIC SKILLS

(Above) Jungle Warfare Training, Ft. Sherman, Panama. (Facing) Rappelling down a waterfall, Panama.

(Above and facing) Jungle Warfare Training, Ft. Sherman, Panama.

A jungle command post, Panama.

"Shoot, move, and communicate." Accurate battlefield coordinates spell the winning difference in warfare.

(Above) Crossing the Rio Chagres, Panama. (Facing) Vertical extraction, Panama. "You only hope the pilot knows that you are a whole lot closer to the deck than he is and doesn't drag you along the treetops," says a Marine.

(Above and facing) Marines at Ft. Sherman, Panama. Modern technology ended one of the infantryman's greatest pleasures: canned
peaches. Now dehydrated fruit comes in plastic bags bearing the
encouraging instructions, "Eat As Is or Reconstitute with Water."

(Above and facing) Crossing the Rio Chagres, Panama, is exhausting work.

(Above and facing) The many faces of Marine Corps excellence.

General P. X. Kelley, at left, and General A. M. Gray, far right, Marine
Corps Commandants, confer at a briefing in 29 Palms, California,
home of the Corps' Desert Warfare Center.

(Above) Training conditions test the mettle of both weapons and men. (Overleaf, pages 82-83) Night Infiltration Course, Camp Lejeune, North Carolina. (Overleaf, pages 84-85) Ft. Sherman, Panama.

OFFICERS AND NCOS

Only Marines serving with the 5th and 6th Regiments are allowed to wear the fourragere, earned by the regiments' heroic actions at the Battle of Belleau Wood, France, during World War I.

There is nothing easy about being an officer of Marines. Extensive, rigorous training is followed by years of regimented duty—with few of the creature comforts to which most civilians are accustomed.

Basic training at the Officer Candidate School (OCS) in Quantico, Virginia, is just as tough, if not tougher, than basic training for enlisted men at the Parris Island and San Diego boot camps.

At Quantico, emphasis is placed on leadership, tactical and academic training, and physical conditioning. The candidates are assigned command positions on a rotating basis. Each rotation is designed to test a man's or woman's ability to lead, and the rigors of the training are usually sufficient to weed out anyone who is not up to the job.

After receiving a commission as a second lieutenant, the officer will then attend The Basic School, also at Quantico, for half a year. The Basic School, commonly referred to as TBS, builds on OCS training. The young lieutenants are drilled in marksmanship; map reading; communications; infantry tactics on the small-unit level; the operation of basic infantry weapons; Marine Corps history and organization; and the basics of close-air support, mechanized operations, amphibious warfare, and other military subjects. Lieutenants are graded on both military knowledge and leadership. It is intense training, and the TBS graduate can command a platoon or similar unit of tanks, amtracs, or artillery. About one-third of all TBS graduates aim for naval aviator wings, and will spend an additional 13-15 months at flight school in Pensacola, Florida.

With the exception of future pilots, a young man or woman joining the Corps can count on being in a command position within ten months of entering Quantico for the first time. An infantry command position is still considered the best possible option for a young lieutenant. Infantry command is a significant consideration in promotions, and most closely fits the

Corps' 200-year-old ideal of the "warrior."

Today's Marine officer is probably as qualified a military professional as any system of training can produce. Continued schooling after basic training ensures that the Marine officer expands his or her skills and knowledge. But Marine officers and senior NCOs are among the first to point out that high training levels can never compensate for lack of experience in combat. No training paradigm can fully portray the accurate, split-second decision-making called for on the battlefield.

At TBS Barracks in Quantico, a plaque quotes the Marines Corps manual: "The special trust and confidence, which is expressly reposed in each officer by his commission, is the distinguishing privilege of the officer corps. It is the policy of the Marine Corps that this privilege be tangible and real; it is the corresponding obligation of the officer corps that it be wholly deserved." Marine Corps officers have no written code of ethics. Each officer must orient himself by means of a large body of general legal and philosophical writings; he must learn to merit the trust and confidence accorded him by his position.

It is this process of acculturation that makes Marine officers a special breed. Codes of conduct are handed down from generation to generation, until they become unwritten, yet formal, law. With every new class of Marine officers graduating from The Basic School, rights and responsibilities are refined.

"It's living tradition," says a Marine major who teaches tactics at TBS. "The fraternity of Marine officers is small. We can afford to forgo regulations. If some

officer is a failure, word will get around fast. This helps us to keep the quality up, with few formalities."

Marine Corps leaders demand instant obedience based on the mutual trust and shared concern for the welfare of the individual. Good leadership is not learned overnight. It must be refined, and most importantly, practiced. Enlisted Marines rapidly form opinions about their commanding officers. They carefully observe how well a leader "takes care" of them, which is not necessarily tied to how well-liked he is personally. "Marines take care of their own," is a tenet of utmost importance to officers.

"If you are low on rations, you share them," explains a captain. "If one of your Marines doesn't have a sleeping bag in his gear but you have one," he says, "it's bad leadership. Sure, it's that Marine's fault to leave the sleeping bag behind. But you are responsible for him."

Good leadership is impossible to fake. A platoon commander is expected to know and care for his men individually. "They will remember that you didn't recall their name," says one lieutenant, who spent close to eight months as a platoon commander with the 2nd Marines. "They expect you to know everything about them. I have spent hours and hours memorizing their records, where they're from, their problems."

Perhaps the most significant comment about the relationship of officers to troops was made by a commandant of the Marine Corps not long after the end of World War I. "The relation between officers and enlisted men should in no sense be that of a superior and inferior nor that of master and servant, but rather that of teacher and scholar," wrote General John A. Lejeune in 1926. "In fact, it should partake of the nature of the relation between father and son, to the extent that officers, especially commanding officers, are responsible for the physical, mental, and moral welfare, as well as the discipline and military training of the young men under their command."

      ★   ★   ★

Much of a young officer's training is conducted by Marine Corps non-commissioned officers (NCOs). Young lieutenants will rely heavily on their NCOs when they get their first command, usually an infantry platoon. NCOs are individuals who have been granted power by their peers; they have risen through the ranks. They are often big, strapping men, immaculately turned out in their uniforms, and utterly self-confident. They are the true mentors of Marine Corps officers.

"NCOs make this Corps run," claims a battalion sergeant major with the 2nd Marines in Camp Lejeune, North Carolina. He stands tall, even when he is seated. His uniform is beautifully pressed — if ironing were an art form, his uniform would be in the Metropolitan Museum of Art. He has dark, glowing skin and a rich, resonant voice with a trace of Mississippi in it.

He "struggled through Parris Island" in the 1950s. Now, some 30 years later, and after Korea, Lebanon in 1958, and two tours of duty in Vietnam, he is ready to retire. "Being an NCO in the Corps is the best of all possible ranks," he says. "No officer can get anything done without you, and you know that it's you who makes it all happen."

Marine NCOs do, in fact, have special power. The basis is both historical and organizational. From its in-ception, the Corps has placed particular emphasis upon individual autonomy. Marine officers are willing to delegate a wider measure of responsibility to their non-commissioned officers than is customary in many other military forces. NCOs are the acknowledged masters of drill and parade. Young officers not only defer to their expertise but willingly submit to being trained, coached, and advised by their subordinates.

In public, NCOs are careful about demonstrating their knowledge and power, but in private they may complain about their superiors. At any time in any NCO club aboard a Marine base, one can hear sergeants complaining about some "stupid" lieutenant, captain, or major. When a new commander arrives, senior sergeants are already fully informed of his or her qualities through the Corps' elaborate intelligence grapevine.

"A good NCO will spot a phony within minutes," says the sergeant major of a Camp Lejeune battalion. "We, as NCOs, will do anything for a good leader, a good officer. But wimps — and trust me, there are wimps in the Corps as everywhere else — will be found out and given a hard time. This is important, because we have to rely on these officers, in peace and in war."

In every U.S. embassy around the world, or consulate where protection is provided, the Marine guards are commanded by a senior NCO. At the U.S. embassy in Paris, for example, a gunnery sergeant commands a detachment of 33 Marines, almost platoon size, which would normally be led by a second lieutenant. NCOs commanding such detachments are often the highest-ranking Marines in the country, with significant diplomatic and public affairs responsibilities.

With the Corps turning more and more to high-technology weapons, NCOs will fill increasingly demanding jobs. Marine aviation provides an excellent example. No Marine airplane can fly without proper maintenance; upkeep of a $33 million fighter like the F/A-18 Hornet requires a high degree of training, proficiency, and experience. In virtually all Marine squadrons, the line responsibility for maintenance is held by senior NCOs.

"It's a fun job," says the maintenance chief of VMA-223, a Harrier jet squadron at Cherry Point, North Carolina. "Sometimes I get downright scared thinking about my young lance corporals playing around with the guts of one of those planes," he says. "But they are tremendously dedicated; they know what they do must be right every time. That sense of responsibility goes all the way up the line."

High technology weaponry has other ramifications for the Corps. The current Marine infantry battalion has some 10 percent fewer Marines, yet close to 25 percent more firepower. Sophisticated and powerful weapons are in the hands of a smaller number of men. Today, a 13-man squad can accomplish far more than ever before. But the sergeants and corporals leading those squads must possess the technical skill and leadership ability to put all this power to use.

Giving NCOs big responsibilities and letting them function as leaders "is one of the secrets of the high quality of Marine NCOs," a tank company first sergeant says. Sergeants, often only 22 years old, routinely command the Corps' main battle tank, the M-60.

For the public, however, the image of the Marine NCO is most often the stereotypical grim, screaming drill instructor wearing a broad-brimmed campaign hat. It is the DI, the first military leader encountered by the raw recruit, who holds perhaps the most awesome responsibility for the future of the Corps. During an 11-week period, he or she is responsible for the training and indoctrination of 70-80 young men or women.

"The drill instructor must be sharp, competent. He must be the epitome of grace, power, and self-assurance. His uniform must be immaculate, from his campaign hat to his glistening brass and shoes," says a colonel. DIs must possess extraordinary tenacity and endurance. During the boot camp training ritual, they will work 70, 80, even 90 hours a week, setting the example for the recruits. DI duty is the toughest peacetime job that the Corps offers.

Marine Corps tradition is rich with the history of NCOs who have earned honors on the battlefield. Most famous is Gunnery Sergeant Dan Daley, who was twice awarded the Medal of Honor. He and other "fighting sergeants" are role models for young Marines.

The halls of the receiving building on Parris Island, where new recruits get their heads shaved, hear lectures about the Uniform Code of Military Justice, and spend their first night in the Corps, are decorated with simple black-and-white pictures of famous Marines, many of them NCOs. The figures stare down from their frames at that nightly parade of new recruits.

"It's like a silent warning and challenge to those kids," says a staff sergeant on duty at receiving. "'Look at us and what we did,' those pictures seem to say. 'You'd better live up to this.'"

(Overleaf, pages 90-91) Marine Corps Air-Ground Combat Center, 29 Palms, California. "A Marine has to learn to fight in every place, desert to Arctic," says an NCO.

(Facing and above) Infantry assault training in the Mojave Desert. Marine air and ground combat arms are fully integrated. Marine pilots routinely serve with infantry battalions as Forward Air Controllers to call in air strikes. (Overleaf, pages 94-95) A Marine Corps A-4 Skyhawk lays down a heavy smoke screen to conceal the movement of armor across the desert plains at 29 Palms, California.

(Above and facing) 29 Palms, California. Artillery is critical for the support of advancing infantry and armor. A CH-53 Super Stallion helicopter brings in a 105mm howitzer.

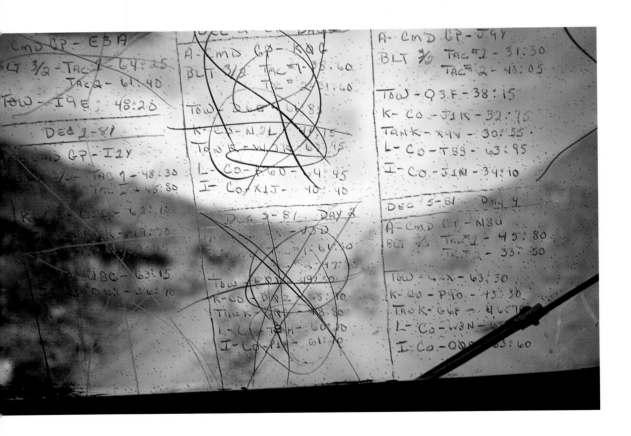

Good communications are essential: a Marine has listed all his radio
codes on his jeep windshield, 29 Palms, California.

"You can spot officers from a long distance away," says a private. "They travel in packs like nuns and lawyers, always with a radio and a map board."

29 Palms, California.

The CH-46 Sea Knight helicopter, capable of carrying up to 20 troops, is the Marine Corps' primary assault and transport helicopter.

(Above and facing) "Our eight-inch gun can deliver quite a punch, up to 30 kilometers away," says a Marine artilleryman at 29 Palms, California.

Near 29 Palms, California, a chaplain conducts service before an improvised altar. "Our chaplain is a very unusual one," says a colonel. "He used to be a grunt, so even serving a new master, he won't let go of his Corps."

Travel in the desert is, at best, slow.

(Facing and overleaf, pages 108-109) Desert
Warfare Training, Mojave Desert.

"I don't care how high-tech we get, we'll still end up sitting around a camp fire waiting for morning," says a Marine officer in the Mojave Desert, California.

Illumination rounds burn over the Bullion Mountains.

ABOARD SHIP

Sailing aboard a warship toward an amphibious landing may sound glamorous. It is not.

"The Navy tries to make it as bad as possible," says a Marine sergeant major aboard the U.S.S. *Guadalcanal*, a helicopter carrier. "They must figure that the more you hate the ship, the Navy chow, the Navy altogether, the more eager you will be to get off, even if the landing beach is heavily defended."

The primary reason for lousy conditions for the Marines is lack of space. Sometimes the misery can begin even before they are on board.

At the end of a major European landing exercise, the Navy was to load Marines back on board the *Guadalcanal* and other vessels in readiness for a move to another operation in northern Germany. The Navy calls this process "backloading."

After waiting around for a day on an empty field —while the Navy considered whether or not to bring their ships into port through heavy fog—some 1,800 Marines, two full battalions, were moved by bus, jeep, and truck to the Danish port of Arhus. A gray Baltic Sea greeted them at the dock—gray sea, gray sky, gray dock, but no large, gray warship. After a full day waiting in light rain and eager for hot food and showers after a week in the field, the Marines grumbled, but settled down. Two Mike-boats, small landing craft that can carry about 20 Marines at a time, droned out of the fog.

"It's going to take two days to backload 1,800 Marines with those bathtubs," comments a staff sergeant.

The crew of the Mike-boats, after long, mysterious deliberations, loaded two groups of Marines and headed out towards the *Guadalcanal*, rumored to be anchored

some three miles out to sea. A hundred yards from the dock one of the Mike-boats developed engine trouble. Both returned, and the Marines disembarked. The Navy crew decided that it would take a while to repair the engine, and darkness was rapidly falling over the Baltic fog.

The Marines were told to settle down for the night on the dock, while the Navy crews took refuge —from the elements and probably from the enraged Marines—in the nearby town.

Next morning the backloading resumed. The engine of the Mike-boat was repaired with suspicious ease. Two additional boats showed up. Twenty hours later, all Marines were aboard the *Guadalcanal*. Questions and speculation ran rampant. Why were only four of the *Guadalcanal's* eight Mike-boats used? Two were out of order, one was dispatched to buy fresh eggs and lettuce, and another was assigned to a Navy photographer to film the backloading, someone claims. But no one seems able to explain why the U.S.S. *Inchon*, a sister ship of the *Guadalcanal*, was tied up at the dock where the Marines were waiting, while the *Guadalcanal* reportedly could not enter port through the fog.

Aboard, the metallic PA system announces, "Now hear this, now hear this. The unique requirement to backload over 1,800 Marines on short notice was met by your boats with speed and enthusiasm. It is a credit to your training program. Well done."

After the Marine laughter dies down, a lieutenant points out that the "unique requirement" was standard operating procedure in any amphibious landing and that the Navy was informed of the exercise several months in advance.

"Normally we get along real well with the Navy," explains a first sergeant, with a hint of irony in his voice, as we enter the hangar deck, wet and loaded down with heavy field packs.

"There goes the neighborhood," a sailor says, eyeing the Marines.

"There's a lot of healthy competition with the Navy," the sergeant continues. "We need each other."

Life aboard ship for the Marines is crowded and, ultimately, boring.

"It's a bit like jail," comments one Marine. "The whole thing is built of steel, there are rigid rules, you can't get out, and everybody wears the same thing."

Conditions aboard ship, of course, have improved tremendously over the centuries. Roman historian Tacitus wrote about Roman warships—the Romans were expert in amphibious warfare—claiming that the ships and their crews could be smelled from miles away. British warships of the 16th and 17th centuries, partially manned by Royal Marines, were also smelly places. Sailors slept on hammocks slung between bulkheads. The men would routinely dislodge vermin from their hardtack by pounding it against the table.

"The troop compartments—oh God, the troop compartments," wrote Martin Russ, a Marine who fought in the Korean War, in 1957. "Understatement of the year: they are crowded. The racks—stretched canvas, designed specifically to avoid any support of the sacroiliac—stand four to six high and are so close, one on top of the other, that one's nose, pelvis, knees, and toes are partially flattened when the man above moves around.

The man in the uppermost tier is usually the most fortunate one, unless he happens to be located under one of the continuously glaring lights of the hold. The troop compartments carry a static odor of sweaty feet and vomit."

Today the troop holds, often way below waterline, are more comfortable. Stretched canvas racks have been replaced with metal boards, covered with a thin mattress. The tiers are 22 inches apart. Each bunk is equipped with a small reading light. The aisles between the bunks are just wide enough to allow one-way traffic. All personal gear is stored in small wall lockers. The air always smells of sweat, shoe polish, germicides, cigarettes, and, when the blowers break down, the foul reek of the heads.

The common holds for the enlisted men, about the size of a standard yellow school bus, contain bunks for 180 men. At night, red safety lights cast a surreal glow over the scene. The tinny blare of Japanese radios and tape recorders—every Marine seems to have at least two—barely drowns out the din of weapons being cleaned, the clamor of commands, the hubbub of sea stories and other fantasies, the clatter of card games, and cloying PA announcements: "Sweepers! Sweepers, man your brooms. Sweep all decks. Sweep her clean!"

The all-metal troop compartments reverberate with every sound. Yet the noise and crowded conditions would be bearable if the Marines had something to keep them occupied.

"Imagine over a thousand healthy, energetic young men crowded together with nothing to do," says a commanding officer. "You start inventing work to keep them busy."

Marines are put to work in the galley and the ship's laundry. There are libraries and classes taught by civilians, but nothing sufficient to fill the many days at sea. A statistically minded corporal informed me that in two weeks of sailing he had won 87 card games, lost 43 card games, drunk 113 cups of coffee, smoked 487 cigarettes, chewed the contents of two packs of Red Man chewing tobacco, run 37 miles on the flight deck, gotten one haircut, and read one detective story.

I discovered the sergeant major, a veteran of 18 cruises, busy in his stateroom completing a model of an 18th-century warship. His house in North Carolina is home port for 17 other such model ships, one for each cruise.

Much time is spent shining and reshining boots. A thorough spit-shine can take more than an hour, depending upon how bored the Marine is. When the flight deck is available, time is spent with physical training. Each Marine quickly learns that 13 times around the flight deck of the *Guadalcanal* equals three miles.

Time is spent cleaning and recleaning gleaming weapons, packing and repacking perfect packs, cutting off imaginary "Irish Pennants" from utility uniforms, and standing in line.

Standing in line is actually pleasurable aboard ship. It is something to do, and provides unlimited opportunities to gossip and complain. Occasions to stand in line are many at sea: post office, barber shop, dispensary, laundry, library, ship stores, disbursing office, chaplain's office, and mess hall.

"Mess hall is best," explains a Marine. "The line moves real slow, you can bitch at the cooks, and it happens three times a day."

Few Marines are eager letter writers; some officers even receive complaints from anxious parents, and will force a Marine to write home. But aboard ship, Marines turn into prolific letter writers, surprising parents, grandparents, aunts, uncles, and girlfriends. "We estimate that we handle three letters and postcards a week from each Marine," claims the mail officer on the *Guadalcanal.*

Your mind seeks anything to keep it occupied. Watching television reruns or reading the skimpy one-page ship's newspaper fills up a little time. You might spend 20 minutes studying a contraption jerry-rigged on a wall locker, a spent round hanging by a string that moves slightly with the rolling of the ship: 10 degrees QUEASY — 15 degrees BARF CITY — 30 degrees ABANDON SHIP.

Real work occupies at least some time — consultations with NCOs or lectures by the battalion commander, who uses an immense playing board to teach tactics. As H-Hour approaches, there are numerous briefings and endless rehearsals. Sometimes there are rehearsals of briefings. Maps require much skill and time; covered front and back with plastic, slowly limned with numerous colored pens, they are pieces of art.

Officers are moderately busier than enlisted men; the higher in rank, the more work they have to do. Marine officers and NCOs, like their naval counterparts, live in comparable luxury. Lieutenants find themselves in "staterooms" containing six or nine racks. There are sinks, mirrors, lines to dry clothing, chairs to sit on, and a PA system. Captains and majors share two-man staterooms, while battalion commanders and higher ranks have a whole room to themselves. Of course, there is peeling paint, sporadic lighting, and constant noise from helicopters landing on the top deck and the ship's engines below.

For many officers time aboard ship is spent waiting. Meals are the high point of the day. Unprompted, the officers rise at five or six in the morning and rush to the wardroom to stand in line for breakfast. Like enlisted men, they wolf their food down; eating rapidly is force of habit. The time between lunch and dinner is often spent getting more sleep. Lieutenants aboard the *Guadalcanal* term those hours MORP, Marine Officers' Rest Period.

Ultimately, a sense of isolation dominates everything. First you lose your sense of time. The ship's belly, uniformly lit, gives no clue as to the time of day or the weather. In a vessel the size of the *Guadalcanal,* you sense hardly any movement. You have to go topside to see if it is light or dark, sunny or overcast. You are cut off from everything. No radio, no newspapers.

A visit to the fantail to practice long-distance tobacco-juice spitting reinforces the sense of isolation. There may be another ship in sight — in all likelihood, a Soviet spy ship, badly camouflaged as a fishing trawler. Someone tells you that you will land in two days at 0545. Somebody else says the operation has been can-celled. No, someone else claims, we will land in three days. Nobody knows for sure.

Practically any event adds excitement or provides raw material for conversation. The night before the landing in Germany, "Flash Gordon" was the film being shown in the wardroom. Two interruptions were the best part of the evening. First, general quarters was sounded. It was only a drill. Ten minutes later, everybody returned to the movie. The second interruption was the chaplain's benediction for the landing, which was nearly drowned out by the sounds of the Pac-Man machine in the corner of the room.

"However much you want to avoid it," says a major, "sometime in your career as a Marine, you will have to spend time aboard ship. It's part of our tradition, and a necessary part of our mission. That doesn't make the experience any better, but it's motivation enough to put up with all this."

Long cruises, such as the traditional six-month deployment in the Mediterranean, are roller coasters of excitement and boredom. Frequent landings in places like Corsica, Sardinia, Sicily, Turkey, or Morocco, alternate with the monotony of life aboard ship.

"You know that this is not forever," says a Marine private spread out on his bunk. "We'll get off sooner or later. I hope sooner."

"Thirteen times around the flight deck of the 'Guad' equals three miles," says a Marine aboard the helicopter carrier LPH-7, U.S.S. *Guadalcanal*.

At Grantangen Fjord, Norway, members of the *Guadalcanal* crew get ready for a helo-borne assault. (Overleaf, pages 118-119) "Amphibious landings," says a Marine officer in Norway, "are our bread and butter." (Overleaf, pages 120-121) The two rotors of the CH-46 Sea Knight create powerful rotor wash.

Marine NCOs figure out the details of getting into a landing zone.

"We'll come over the beach, we'll come from the sky, we'll come any way we can surprise the enemy," says a Marine on maneuvers in Denmark.

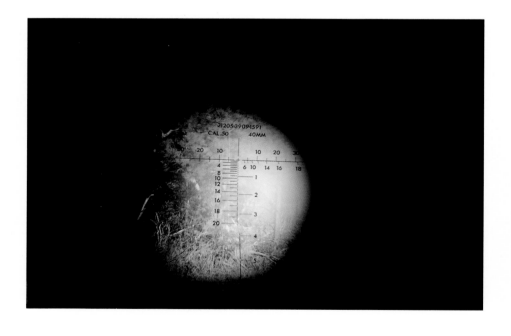

(Above and facing) "A tank is an awesome weapon," comments a
tank commander. "But our main job is to support the grunt."

Marine M-60 tanks on the move in Germany.

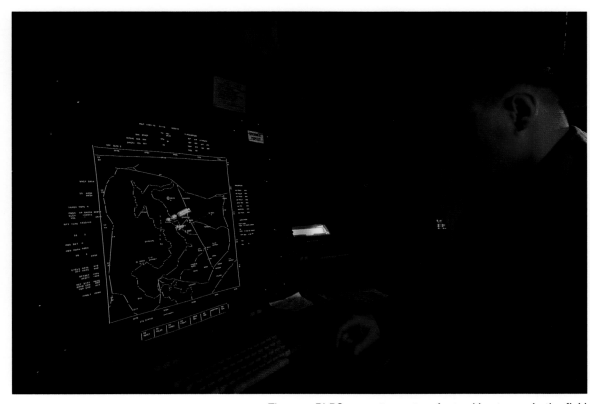

The new PLRS computer system for tracking troops in the field enables unit commanders to monitor and control troop movements much as a flight controller monitors planes approaching an airport.

WINTER WAR

Amtracs navigate a Norwegian fjord.

The U.S. Marine Corps must contend with extremes. Jungles, deserts, and the Arctic Circle are among the areas where they might be expected to fight. In a confrontation with the Soviets, U.S. Marines, along with British and Dutch Marines, could be called upon to reinforce the small but tough Norwegian army in the far north of Norway's 2,000-mile-long reach.

Soviet troops, NATO planners expect, would cross the Soviet-Norwegian border some 250 miles north of the Arctic Circle. Their objective would be to seize the large airfield at Bardufoss, along with the vital areas of Finnmark and Troms. The Soviet Northern Fleet is based at Murmansk; control of northern Norway would allow the Soviets not only to protect their fleet, but also to interfere with NATO shipping between the United States, Iceland, and the United Kingdom.

World War II proved that control of Norway is important. The German battleship *Tirpitz* was able to occupy a sizable portion of the Royal Navy simply by sitting and waiting in a Norwegian fjord. "World War III cannot be won in Finnmark," says a Norwegian general, "but it can very well be lost here."

Conducting an amphibious landing in the Arctic Circle, with or without enemy opposition, is a next-to-impossible endeavor. But Marines seem to take pride in coping with environments that push human endurance to its limits. Northern Norway is such an environment. There are no true beaches to land on. Narrow fjords are bordered by stark mountain ranges rising more than 3,000 feet above the water. The number of fjords that can be penetrated by landing forces is small; many are too shallow and others dead-end in steep cliffs. An amphibious ship must navigate treacherous waters to reach a point where a force can be landed. Limited in its ability to maneuver or to get an early "fix" on incoming aircraft, a ship is a sitting duck.

Then there is the weather. For six months of the year, the land is covered with snow and ice. During the long Arctic night that occurs in winter, sunlight disappears altogether, and temperatures range from five degrees Fahrenheit to −60 degrees. Because of the Gulf Stream current, the fjords rarely freeze, but strong winds instantly turn water droplets into ice. Spilled water freezes within a few seconds.

"Winter is never over up here," explains a Norwegian.

Probably the only aspect of northern Norway that devolves to the benefit of the Marines is the terrain. Except for its many frozen lakes, where the ice is strong enough to support tanks, helicopters, and heavy artillery, Norway offers no open areas. Mountain piles upon mountain, with no open plain through which a large army with a contingent of armor can sweep.

"If the Russians come," says a Royal Marines major, "they will have to come more or less in single file through one of the few mountain passes in the Finnmark." The terrain virtually dictates a guerilla war of small, isolated units operating independently. "U.S. Marines are the type of troops we need up here," says a Norwegian general. "The terrain is tailored to the type of war where Marines excel."

Close-air support, however, is crucial in a terrain that is difficult for tanks and artillery. Only one airfield, Bardufoss, is suited for conventional jets. If that field were lost, Marines would have to depend on aircraft carriers stationed in the Atlantic. The Soviets, on the other hand, have 16 large airfields close to the border.

"This area presents another argument for the Harrier," says a Marine major. "VSTOL (Vertical/Short Take-Off and Landing) planes are an absolute must." The AV-8B Harrier could take off and land on the ice at many of the larger lakes.

But cold weather seriously restricts flying operations. Planes and helicopters on the ground must be de-iced frequently, a time-consuming operation. Moreover, fewer Marines can be carried on each helicopter. In a "normal" environment, a Marine will carry a combat load of 50-60 pounds. In the Arctic, counting his special winter clothing, a Marine's combat load increases to 120 pounds, and takes up about twice as much space. As a result, helicopters must make numerous trips to move a relatively small number of troops.

On land mobility is severely limited. Loaded with heavy survival gear, a Marine will have great difficulty moving at the speeds to which he is accustomed. Snowshoes help, but progress remains painfully slow. On open march across relatively flat land, a Marine squad can take more than an hour to cover one mile. Deep snow and heavy equipment can slow things down to a crawl.

The boots the men are issued for this environment "are great to stand in," says a Marine gunnery sergeant. "Your feet will never get cold." The boots are white, made of heavy insulated rubber, and are commonly referred to as "Mickey Mouse boots." Rated to −65 degrees, they weigh five pounds each. "Marching in those things is tough."

Changing socks and removing or replacing bulky layers of clothing become difficult, time-consuming tasks in the Arctic environment. Touch metal with your bare hands and your skin will freeze to it. Adjusting sights on a rifle or reloading a magazine while wearing thick gloves is maddeningly slow. "Up here it takes six times as long to set up a battery of 105s (105mm howitzers) as it takes anywhere else," says an artillery commander.

Overall, the Marines do surprisingly well. "We are not specially trained for arctic warfare," says a Marine colonel. "Instead we train for any possible and probable contingency. Our ability to do well in a variety of extremes makes us unique among most other armed forces."

Norwegian and British officers are quick to compliment the U.S. Marines. "That such a general-purpose unit as the Corps can come from a warm climate, land here, and do well against specialized arctic troops should give the Russians something to think about," says a Norwegian officer.

★　　★　　★

D-Day. The list of Arctic gear for U.S. Marines is truly astonishing. For Norway it includes one standard sleeping bag; one arctic shell for the sleeping bag; one roll of foam sheet for insulation; one pack, double the usual size; one pack frame; one set of straps for the pack; one cold-weather canteen; one cold-weather canteen cup; one cold-weather canteen cover; one set of "782" gear (web belt and suspenders); one steel helmet, one steel helmet liner; one steel helmet cover, camouflaged (white); one watch cap, wool, black; one wool scarf; one waterproof bag; one first-aid kit; one entrenching tool with carrier; one pair of arctic boots, white; one sleeping shirt, heavy wool; one set of long thermal underwear; one pair of insulated trousers; one pair of insulation liners for insulated trousers; one pair of white outer shells, top and bottom, cotton; one coat liner, insulated; one coat; one cover (hood) with fur; one cover with flaps to close under the chin; one set of leather gloves with wool liners; one set of mittens; one set of mittens with separate trigger fingers; one set of liners with trigger fingers; one set of white glove covers with opening for trigger finger; one set of sunglasses; one gas mask; one one-liter steel thermos; one sea bag to contain all these items. Added to this gear are ammunition pouches, pistol holsters, a rifle, 200 rounds of ammunition, a bayonet knife, grenades, a flashlight, a compass, and food to last for one or two days.

The gear weighs close to 200 pounds. It takes me 20 minutes to put all my clothes on. My girth has increased by about 150 percent, and all the Marines, dressed as I am, look like weird prehistoric monsters. The U.S.S. *Guadalcanal,* in a fjord near Bjerkvik, is rolling and pitching in rough seas. As soon as I have donned all my gear, I start sweating. I fill my thermos with hot, black Navy coffee.

"It's the last you'll get for some days," says a Marine.

I wait for close to two hours to go ashore. Flight operations are alternately cancelled and started up again.

"The wind is too strong, 80 knots," somebody says.

"You will survive 30 seconds if you go into the drink," says a Marine pilot. Pilots wear insulated rubber suits that will keep them alive for several minutes in the arctic waters.

Finally, there is a signal that a Huey helicopter will take me and several Marines ashore. After that, flight operations will be shut down for good. I struggle up the ladders, getting a push or two from behind so that I don't fall over backwards, pulled down by my overweight pack. I push the Marine in front of me. The hatches are too narrow for us with all our gear; we have to squeeze through. In the Huey, the seat belt is not long enough to fit around me.

It's a rough ride. The winds push the helicopter around like a feather. We land on a small lake, the ice smooth as a mirror. I get out of the helicopter and try to walk. The wind blows me off my feet. Two Marines next to me also fall down.

"Stand up and let yourself be blown across the ice," yells a voice coming from a snow drift on the bank of the lake. After several tries I get up, use my pack as a sail, and glide across the ice.

A platoon of Marines is hidden in snowdrifts near the lake, awaiting transportation inland. The platoon commander makes them jump up and down, walk

around, run—anything to keep warm. I am grateful for every ounce of clothing on my body, all five layers. I drink some foul-tasting coffee from my thermos. My eyes tear. The tears freeze to my skin.

The wind blows a 4,893-pound, 105mm howitzer straight across the ice towards us. It's impossible to stand up when it gusts.

Finally a truck comes to take us to the front. After a long ride, we are dropped off in another snowdrift in the middle of nowhere. Here, there is no wind. Moving around makes me feel hot. I open my parka. Some Marines have removed their woolen caps.

D+1. In a clearing, Marines try to make coffee. Some 20 of them, all in white, huddle around a tiny stove trying to melt snow. I am amazed at how long it takes, and how much snow is required to get a gallon of water. The coffee is great. I follow the example of an older Marine on his second tour in the Arctic and combine dehydrated chicken noodle soup with cocoa and coffee.

"I love it," says a PFC. "It's why I joined the Marine Corps."

His humor affirms the excellent morale. Most of the Marines seem to enjoy the rough environment. I examine something called "Orange Beverage Bar" and decide against consumption. It is part of a packet called "Assault Menu #3, Prototype." Arctic rations are very good, especially compared to standard rations. We have chocolate bars, iced tea, and beef jerky. We are instructed to eat well and as often as possible to keep our strength up. I try trading the arctic rations with British Royal Marines; they turn me down, but offer me some of their chocolate candy.

"I'll never see the day when our allies prefer our rations over theirs," says a gunnery sergeant. Even the Norwegian troops evince little interest in our "Assault Menu #3, Prototype." They prefer their cold, canned, greasy sardines.

It is nighttime, and I am amazed at how well I can see. The sky is dark, but there is just a touch of moonlight, which is reflected by the snow.

D+2. The tent is incredibly small and shared by ten Marines. In the center is a stove, and everyone sleeps with his feet pointed toward it. There is no room to turn over. Bodies press from either side.

It takes a long time to break down the tent. Anything that you have to do with your bare hands, in fact, is painful. Each of us carries a section of the tent, diamond-shaped pieces of canvas or tent poles, over to a fiberglass sled the Marines call the "poke."

One of the lieutenants enjoys putting up the tent so much that he refuses to let anyone help when we arrive at a new bivouac. Two gunnery sergeants and four corporals stand around watching the officer do the work. Spirits are good. There is much serious talk about liquor, liberty, and women.

The tent stove has an open flame. Somebody has to watch it all night long. Carbon monoxide fumes could asphyxiate everyone. Or the tent might catch fire.

I pour water into a brown plastic bag labeled "Scalloped Potatoes with Pork." This is "Assault Menu #2, Prototype." The material is rock-hard.

"You have to crumble it up first," says a lance corporal. He demonstrates by pounding a similar package with his boot. The pulverized material is gray and swells up with water. It also swells in my stomach for hours.

A night assault on an "enemy" position held by Italian NATO troops is scheduled. We move in the darkness, and the march is slow. We are allowed to leave most of our gear behind; a truck will pick it up later. It's a relief to be unburdened of the heavy gear.

Somehow we get lost. According to the map, we are located atop a 1,340-meter mountain. We are standing on a frozen lake. Everything is so white, it's easy to lose your sense of direction. We heat water and make coffee. The lieutenant radios for directions. It turns out that we are in the right location after all. The attack goes well. We trade rations with the Italians after our "assault." The Italians get red wine every day.

D+3. I attend a tactical briefing, complete with map and pointer. I start to understand what all my moving around with the infantry over the past two days has been about. The Marines have been "leapfrogging," trying to catch the opposition by surprise. Helicopters move troops close to the front; infantry follows on foot. It's fast, efficient, and seems to confuse the Norwegians, who have a hard time coping with these "vertical envelopment" tactics. It's impressive to see the effect a single battalion can have. The firepower in the hands of an individual Marine is immense. Provided that it is well deployed, a battalion can have tremendous impact.

The briefing takes place at the 36th Marine Expeditionary Unit (MEU) headquarters, set up next to a mountain. All tents and vehicles are well dug in. The MEU commander has a tent at the end of a deep snow trench. Those waiting to talk to the commander stand outside in the snow.

Suddenly, British Harriers, working for the "enemy," attack headquarters. We are all dead.

"They came so fast, hidden by that mountain range," says a Marine pilot, "that radar wouldn't pick them up, and by the time you see them, it's too late for antiaircraft missiles to engage them. Isn't the Harrier great?"

A helicopter from the *Guadalcanal* lands in a whirlwind of ice and snow. Painted gray, it's called "Candy Cane" for its striped tail insignia. A Marine trades a pack of cigarettes for a fresh loaf of bread.

I go back to the infantry. Word comes that "the King" will visit us. There is much discussion about which king it will be, what to say to the king, and why he is coming in the first place. The lieutenant explains that King Olaf V of Norway is expected and that he used to compete in the Olympics. The Marines are impressed. They debate how to set up an honor guard in the snow. The king never comes.

D+4. I take refuge in a cabin near a lake. In the brief Arctic summer, it's used as a recreational club. A Marine corporal, a photographer for the Camp Lejeune newspaper, accompanies me. We find that two Royal Marines already occupy the cabin; they have turned on the heat and the juke box is playing. There's a pool table, but none of us has any Norwegian coins. The Royal Marines man a refueling station for helicopters that set down in front of the cabin. Just the two of them, and a fuel truck. Refueling here saves their helicopters a long trip back to the ship.

We find coffee and candles. "There is nothing wrong with using the cabin," explain the Royal Marines, who come to Norway every winter. I tell them that in the U.S. this would be considered breaking and entering and that we could be arrested. In Norway it is the law — soldiers in a "combat" zone can use buildings, and civilians are expected to take them into their houses.

I return to MEU headquarters. The "war" is going well for the Marines. Some officers are complaining about the rules that ensure that the Norwegians "win" in the end. "The outcome was fixed a year ago," says a staff officer. "But it's good training for the troops."

I meet Marines from Bravo Company, 1st Battalion, 25th Marines, a reserve outfit based in Manchester, New Hampshire. They are cold-weather specialists, training more than half the year in Maine, New Hampshire, and Vermont. "They are the best Marine unit here," says their Norwegian liaison officer, impressed by their skiing ability. The entire company moves on skis, not snowshoes, and competes in mobility with the Norwegian troops.

It is Sunday and the whole exercise shuts down for two hours to allow the Norwegian Army, which is unionized, to attend church. We wait and talk, drinking hot coffee mixed with chicken noodle soup. I find that I am developing a taste for the combination. There is talk about the Soviet units who sometimes go through winter training wearing only their great coats. The frigid conditions here would hardly affect them, but the Marines are confident that they would "kick the shit" out of the Soviets. It's as if the difficult terrain, the snow and ice, even the prototype arctic menus, have boosted morale and confidence.

(Overleaf, pages 134-135) "The amtrac is what makes the Corps the Corps. It's a heavily armored troop carrier that swims," says a U.S. Marine in Norway.

"The Roman legions had similar maps for their camps," says a
Marine. "Nothing really changes in war."

On maneuvers in Norway, 200 miles north of the Arctic Circle, communications are difficult. "Mountains block out radios and units get lost all the time," says an officer.

(Above and facing) Marine Corps exercises in Norway. "It gets so cold that your eyelids freeze shut," a Marine says.

(Facing) Movement is difficult for troops wearing the bulky layers of clothing necessary for survival in the Arctic. (Above) A 105mm howitzer battery is hidden under camouflage netting.

Canadian soldiers and U.S. Marines protect a mountaintop landing zone in Norway as a Royal Marine helicopter lands with supplies.

ONCE A MARINE, ALWAYS A MARINE

Dress-blue uniform.

"Among all the honors," wrote General John A. Lejeune, the 13th Commandant of the Marine Corps, "among all the postings, promotions, medals, that have been accorded me, the one in which I take the most pride is to be able to say, 'I am a Marine.'"

Talking with a Marine who has not worn a uniform in 30 years can often be more revealing about the Corps' unique qualities than speaking with active-duty Marines. Marines rarely lose their fierce loyalty to the Corps; retiring the uniform seems to reinforce commitment. Some call the Corps a religion; others call it a brotherhood or fraternity where "the highest recommendation of a man is the fact that he is a Marine."

There is not the slightest doubt in a Marine's mind that his or her Corps represents the elite of the elite. This opinion is shared by many non-Marines. Few will deny that Marine Corps service commands instant respect.

"Mention that you are a Marine, and you get all kinds of reactions—awe, respect, snide comments, shock," says a former Marine, now editorial-page editor of a prominent Midwestern newspaper. "But whatever the reaction may be, you can always detect a slight note of concern that 'maybe this guy is real bad and I better watch out,' which can come in handy for a newspaperman working with uncooperative sources."

In the newsroom of a Louisiana weekly paper a style rule is prominently posted on a bulletin board: "Marines are always uppercase; sailors, soldiers, and airmen are lower case. Reporters ignoring this rule will be fined $5." The man who runs the paper is a slender, precise, epicene former Marine. He served in Vietnam in 1966-67, where he was awarded two Purple Hearts, one Silver Star, and two Bronze Stars.

"I sometimes wonder," the publisher says, brushing back a lock of hair, "what the Marine Corps did to get this lifelong hold on me. In Nam we used to say USMC stands for 'Uncle Sam's Misguided Children' or 'Unlimited Shit, Mass Confusion.' Today, I would beat anybody to within an inch of his life if he were to make some off-color comment about my Corps."

Celebrated defense attorney F. Lee Bailey was once PFC Bailey, USMC. Author William Manchester, a former Marine who fought in the Pacific, says that he developed the discipline to write while he was in the Corps. To get out of a tight spot, Marine Art Buchwald often resorted to humor. U.S. Senator Adlai E. Stevenson Jr., whose office was adjacent to that of retired USMC colonel Senator John Glenn, once commanded a Marine Corps tank in Korea.

Many Marines have gained prominence as actors and athletes. Glenn Ford was a Marine Corps sergeant. MacDonald Carey, who played a Marine Corps officer in the movie *Wake Island,* later became a real-life Marine private. Lee Marvin, as PFC Marvin, 24th Marines, fought on Kwajalein and Eniwetok, and was wounded at Saipan. George C. Scott, unforgettable in the role of General George Patton, served for years as a Marine Corps member of the White House Honor Guard. Actors Hugh O'Brien, Steve McQueen, and George Peppard were also Marines. Boxers Gene Tunney, Leon Spinks, and Ken Norton served in the Corps, as did Ted Williams of the Boston Red Sox, who flew 37 combat missions in Korea, and baseball player Hank Bauer, who was awarded a Bronze Star and a Purple Heart.

Circuit-court judges, editorial-page editors, chiefs of police, bank presidents, academic deans—the Marine Corps presence is found across America. Yet perhaps it is in the corporate community that Marines have left their biggest mark. More than one-third of the top executives at America's Fortune 500 companies have served in the U.S. Marine Corps.

* * *

The corporate scene at the polished oak bar is pure power, New York style. Drinks are hard and straight up. Virtually everyone at the bar is a man. They are tanned, even now, in February. Their dark suits are elegant and expensive; their shirts, white; the neckties, subdued. Attorneys, investment bankers, media executives, traders, and corporate moguls, they are enjoying an after-work drink before catching trains to the golden suburbs of Westchester and Fairfield counties.

The president of a major public relations firm fits right in. His firm represents giant corporations, even foreign countries. Thirty-five years ago, however, his world was limited to Korea, where he carried an M-1 rifle and slogged through ice and snow.

Why did he join the Corps? "My father told me to stay away from the Army. I also liked the Marine uniform. I thought I could impress the girls with the dress blues."

He laughs, then calls Parris Island, where grueling Marine training takes place, "the best possible business school ever invented.

"I credit my success to a lot of hard work and a good bit of Marine Corps chutzpa," he says. He muses for a moment, studying his empty glass. "Best thing that ever happened to me, being a Marine."

★   ★   ★

Patriotic music, rock, punk, and soul are on the program of the Marion, Ohio, high-school band playing at homecoming one cool September afternoon. An audience of parents, teachers, brothers, and sisters sit shivering on the bleachers. The band begins the familiar refrain of the Marines' Hymn. Five men stand: the principal of the school, ramrod straight; the father of a football player, looking apologetically at his surprised wife; and three younger men whose unkempt appearance would land them straight in the brig if they were still on active duty. Each is a former Marine. Instinct,

training, and pride compel them to their feet to pay tribute.

★   ★   ★

The academic world seems a far cry from the regimented world of Marines—gleaming uniforms, strict regulations.

The bearded philosophy professor sits sipping herbal tea in his crowded office, decorated with Communist flags "obtained" in Bulgaria, the blackboard full of incomprehensible mathematical formulas, books piled everywhere. It is difficult to imagine him as a Marine Corps artillery officer.

His introduction to the Marines was NROTC training at his university. Six rough weeks at Quantico strengthened his commitment.

"We were shown Marine Corps life. It wasn't pleasant. But there was no hype. The Marines stressed only one thing. 'If you want to join us, prove that we need you,' they said. 'We don't promise anything.'"

"What's so special about the Corps?" I ask him.

"It has all the values a military organization should have in a democracy," he replies. "'The enemy is whomever the President designates as such,' the Commandant told us. That clear sense of values and purpose is impressive."

He sits up straight and gazes out the window of his office. "If there is a way for me to serve the Corps, I would gladly do it."

★   ★   ★

There are many former Marines in the New York Police Department, but probably only one who plays the bagpipes. On St. Patrick's Day he dons his kilt and marches down Fifth Avenue in the NYPD pipe band, playing the Marines' Hymn as they pass a group of Marines on upper Fifth Avenue.

His dream had been to join the Marine Corps Band in Washington, D.C. "They told me that I didn't meet their standards of musical excellence. So I became a grunt."

He carried his bagpipes in Vietnam. "They made my pack kind of heavy at times, but it was good to have them." One Marine Corps birthday, he shared fruitcake from rations and played the Marines' Hymn on his bagpipes, in the middle of a jungle landing zone. "Scared a lot of birds, I guess."

He spent four years with the Corps before changing uniforms to become a member of "New York's finest."

"When I left the Corps, I needed a job. The only real training I had was in small-unit tactics. My drill instructor at Parris Island had gone into the NYPD, and he helped me get in," says the former Marine, who now roams the lower East Side, looking for drug pushers, "but the discipline in this outfit is a real joke by Marine Corps standards."

*   *   *

Bees make good honey all around Waycross, Georgia. The sweet syrup tastes of orange blossoms and eucalyptus and can be bought for a dollar or two a pint at any roadside stand coming north from Jacksonville, Florida, on Route 1. The Okefenokee Swamp, known as the "trembling earth" of south Georgia, starts just a few miles below Waycross.

His stand is built with plywood and old tar paper. A rocking chair, a rusty set of scales, and a 1969 John Deere wall calendar make up the shack's only ornamentation. Outside stands a Ford pickup of indeterminate age, a 55-gallon drum filled with water, and a bleached sign that reads, "PEACHES 35¢." The stand would be indiscernible from the many other honey stands along Route 1 were it not for the colors of both the United States of America and the U.S. Marine Corps that are flown in front. The man who runs the stand enlisted in the Corps in October 1943, the day after he turned 17. He trained, as did all black servicemen during the days of segregation, at Montford Point in Camp Lejeune, North Carolina. "I didn't mind in those days," he says. "That's the way it was if you wanted to serve."

In a worn leather cover he carries his honorable discharge papers, his World War II Victory Medal, and his two Purple Hearts. On Okinawa he lost a hand. "That's what this one is for," he says, holding up one of the Purple Hearts, "and the other one is for that." He indicates a mean-looking scar on his remaining hand. "Was lucky, though, could have lost both."

While a VFW post sits several miles to the north, he has never attended a meeting. Each Memorial Day, however, he and another Montford Point boot camp veteran watch the parade on Main Street. "We stand up real straight and salute," he says. "Want people to know that I was a Marine, been places, fighting for this country, been earning my benefits."

He glances at the Marine Corps flag outside his stand. "I loves the Marines," he says. "I loves the Marines real good."

(Overleaf, pages 148-149) Beirut, Lebanon. "At first it was a pretty good life and nobody paid much attention to us," says a Marine.

Beirut, Lebanon. "When the shelling started we built trenches real quick," says a Marine. "Soon it looked like a bad dream from World War I."

150

A Marine sniper plots targets in Beirut.

Sergeant Major Frederick Douglass rides shotgun for his colonel
in Beirut, Lebanon. He was killed in 1983, 11 days after this photograph was made.

A fortified outpost in Beirut.

"Fire Mission!" In Beirut, Lebanon, Marines run to man 60mm mortars.

Shrapnel from a Soviet 122mm mortar.

(Facing) In Beirut, this bunker and a nearby combat outpost are taking fire. Shells have seriously wounded a Marine in the outpost. The company commander calls in fire to relieve the outpost while he organizes a medical evacuation.

Captain: Roger...do you want them to drop closer to your position?

Outpost: Roger.

Captain: I will tell them to drop 200 meters...tell battalion to drop from 250 to 200...hey, Whiskey, try another round, Willie Peter, over.

Mortars: Stand by.

Corpsman: Can he tell us what kind of blood loss he has?

Captain: Tango One, this is Kilo Charlie, hey Doc, how much blood loss has your patient had, over.

Corpsman: He will be fairly conscious...five milligrams of morphine...

Captain: Tango One, this is Kilo Charlie. You are getting your fire mission.

Corpsman: He already got his morphine...that's all he needs.

Captain: Roger 60, fire, Willie Peter, over...this is Kilo Charlie.

Mortars: This is fire mission.

Captain: Roger, right by 50 drop 100.

Mortars: Roger.

Captain: Right 50, drop on zero zero...do you see anything to your south?

Mortars: Roger that.

Captain: Roger. OK, get on to the south.

Mortars: Let me get the adjustment...stand by.

Captain: Roger, this is Kilo Charlie, left 100, add 300.

Mortars: Roger, left one zero zero, at 300.

Corpsman: The only thing I worry about is, I mean it is going to take an act of Congress to get him out.

Marine: We could get a helo in!

Captain: We get a shot out on the 60s yet?

Mortars: As soon as he gets the adjustment.

Captain: That's the one we gave you...did this just go out?

Mortars: One round for adjustment.

Captain: Tango One, Kilo Charlie, we're in the process of getting all those adjusted...Tango One, this is Kilo Charlie...getting ready to fire...

Corpsman: Can you get social security and blood type?

Outpost: It's Lopez, his social and blood type need to be relayed.

Captain: Fire for effect...fire, fire seven eight four, two six two one.

Corpsman: Blood type?

Captain: Tango One, this is Kilo Charlie, you should have a splash on a 60 Mike Mike.

Outpost: Roger that.

Captain: Tango One, Kilo Charlie, are you positive you got the 60 Mike Mike? Did they get a splash yet...we are going to have a repeat of that...

Mortars: You want Willie Pete?

Captain: Roger that.

Mortars: That's a Roger.

Captain: Tango One, be advised our last shot was a Willie Pete...

Outpost: Roger, direct hit, fire for effect, over.

Captain: Roger that, fire for effect, over.

The Marine was safely evacuated.

(Above) Standing guard, Beirut University, Lebanon. (Overleaf, pages 158-159) Beirut, Lebanon. The Lebanese set up a shack to sell soft drinks, T-shirts, and batteries.

CORPS Exchange

(Above and facing) Beirut, Lebanon, October 1983.

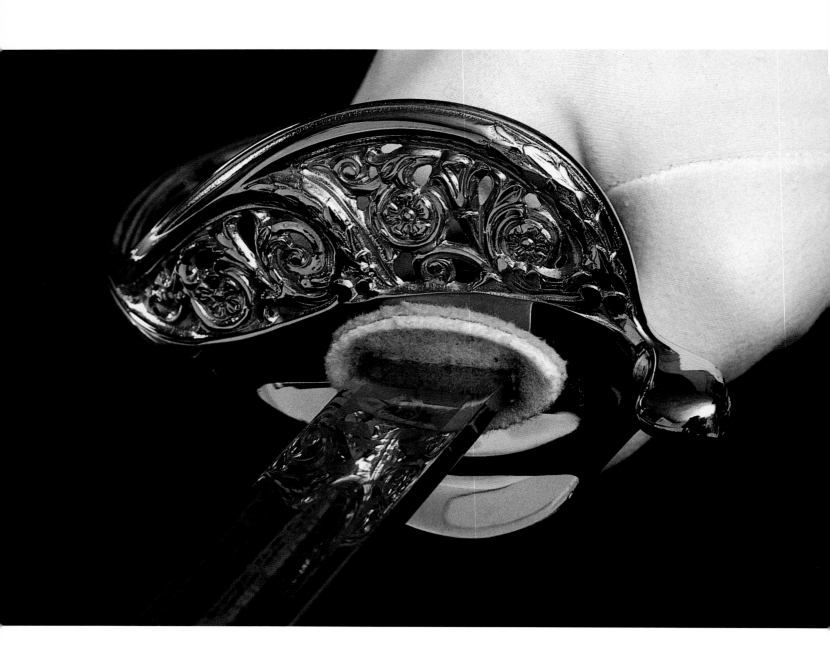

Hilt, Marine NCO sword.

APRICOTS: A GLOSSARY

In an efficient, drab NCO club on a West German army base in Schleswig-Holstein, six Marine officers and some civilians are eating sausages and drinking beer, talking about the operation just completed. They discuss the usual foul-ups, the problems with supply, and the confusion. They discuss rations in great detail—how to make "field" Virginia ham using fruit cocktail and ham slices, for example.

"I heard a superstition that I'd never heard before," says one of the civilians, "that you shouldn't eat apricots in—"

"That's not a superstition, it's a fact," says a tank officer.

"It's a fact, it's a fact," is the chorus of other officers.

"If you eat apricots while on a tank or amtrac, that vehicle is going down," admonishes the tank officer. "I don't know why, but it happens. It's a scientific fact.

"I had a lance corporal who was my loader. He ate a can of apricots from rations. Then moving down the road in my tank, we were hauling along, and b-r-r-o-o-m, the track separated from the tank. We started fixing it and it came out that the lance corporal had eaten apricots. I felt like beating that boy within an inch of his life.

"The first thing we do now, when we get our rations," the tank officer says, "the gunny and I go through them, and if there are apricots, we throw them away. I know it sounds stupid. I thought it was stupid when I first heard about it."

He says the "apricot curse" first manifested itself in Vietnam. He recites incident after incident, where tanks threw track, broke integral pins or bearings, or had engine trouble. In each case, apricots were a factor.

Fact or not, the apricot curse is part of Marine language. It is a rich language, much of which is unprintable. Marine discourse presents a wealth of idiom that tells a tale of forgotten wars, recent conflicts, and the naval heritage of the Corps. Learning to talk like a Marine can only be achieved properly by going through boot camp. What follows here is a glossary of Marine Corps terms for the amateur.

AWS. Amphibious Warfare School, an obligatory course for all recently promoted captains. AWS is one of many schools at the Marine Corps Combat Development Center in Quantico, Virginia, including the Command and Staff College (for majors and lieutenant colonels), the Staff NCO Academy, The Basic School, the Sniper School, and the Sergeant Majors Academy. Quantico is the "college" of the Corps.

APRICOTS. It is common knowledge among members of the Corps that crewmen eating apricots will disable a tracked vehicle of any kind.

AYE, AYE, SIR. Correct form to acknowledge a direct order. It is a naval custom. "Yes, sir," is used in response to a direct question.

THE BASIC SCHOOL (TBS). A six-month school for just-commissioned second lieutenants. At Quantico, young officers are taught basic military know-how.

BIVOUAC. A somewhat archaic term for a camp area in the field.

BLOUSE. The Marine Corps uniform coat, a common term in English-speaking navies. The coat of the USMC combat utility uniform is referred to as the "jacket."

BLUE BOOK. A list of officers, published each year, that lists seniority standing and recent promotions.

BOOT. Derogatory term for a recruit or someone who is junior to the Marine speaking.

BOOT CAMP. The Marine Corps Recruit Training Depots at Parris Island, South Carolina, and San Diego, California. Boot camp is often mentioned as the experience that differentiates Marines from soldiers and sailors.

BRIG. A jail "aboard" a Marine base.

BULKHEAD. Marines refer to walls as "bulkheads," ceilings as "overheads," windows as "portholes," floors as "decks," hallways as "passageways," doors as "hatches," and stairs as "ladders." These are naval terms. Marines use them whether they are aboard ship or on shore.

BUNK. Naval term for a bed, although Marines also use the term "rack." They will never refer to a bed as a bed.

CH. Cargo Helicopter, as in CH-53 Super Stallion or CH-46 Sea Knight.

CMC. Commandant of the Marine Corps.

CORPSMAN. Marine and naval term for "medic," although referring to a corpsman as a medic is considered almost an insult. Marine corpsmen are enlisted naval personnel assigned to serve with the Corps. Often referred to as "Doc" by Marines, corpsmen have earned a solid reputation for never letting their men down. Several corpsmen have earned the Medal of Honor for coming to the aid of Marines under heavy fire.

COVER. Any form of headgear other than a helmet.

DI. The Drill Instructor is the most feared man or woman in a young Marine's life. For up to 11 weeks, recruits are under the strict care of their DIs, and few Marines ever forget the experience. A DI has one of the toughest jobs in the Corps. He or she is charged with molding a young civilian into a proud Marine, a task that requires dedication (80-hour work weeks are common), care, sternness, and a first-rate mind.

FAC. A Forward Air Controller is a pilot serving with infantry units who is responsible for properly coordinating close-air support with ground action. FACs are the link between Marine infantry and Marine aircraft.

FMF. Fleet Marine Force. The FMF is divided into two segments: FMFPac (Pacific) and FMFLant (Atlantic). Commanded by a lieutenant general, each FMF has its own ground troops (one or two divisions) and air wing (one or two air wings). Almost 122,000 of the 197,200 active-duty Marines serve under the FMF, which is often referred to simply as "the fleet." A "gung-ho" corpsman might call himself an "FMF Corpsman." Tall tales beginning, "As we say in the fighting Fleet Marine Force...," are common.

FIELD DAY. Any major cleanup—the whole base, a company headquarters, or a single Marine's personal gear.

FIELD MEET. An all-day competitive sports event with many cans of beer.

FIRE TEAM. The second-smallest tactical unit in the Corps. The smallest tactical unit is the individual rifleman. Three Marine riflemen make up a fire team.

GALLEY. Kitchen. Marines use the word both on land and sea.

GEAR LOCKER. A well-secured storage room used for all types of gear, including weapons. It is not a foot locker.

GO ASHORE. May be applied to a range of activities,

including landing on a beach or leaving a military base to go to town.

GRUNT. A Marine infantryman. Any Marine carrying a rifle becomes a grunt when he is in the field, regardless of his military occupational specialty.

GUNG-HO. Chinese term for "working together." Introduced by Brigadier General Evans Carlson, the phrase was first used in World War II by Marine Raider Battalions. Carlson served as an observer with Mao Tse-Tung's 8th Route Army in China in 1939-40. Impressed with Chinese teamwork, he infused the same spirit in his 2nd Raider Battalion. Often misinterpreted as "hard-charging," gung-ho is better understood as the team spirit pervasive in Marine Corps life.

GUNNER. Old naval term applied to warrant officers. The term dates from the days when non-commissioned officers were promoted to warrant-officer status in recognition of their special knowledge of naval guns. Warrant officers whose specialty is weapons still wear an exploding bomb on their collars, the last remnant of the original term, "Gunner," which now applies to any warrant officer, male or female.

GUNNERY SERGEANT. A unique rank in America's armed forces, gunnery sergeant (E-7) is considered by many Marines to be the most prestigious of the enlisted ranks in the Corps. Called the "gunny," the gunnery sergeant is the key link between senior enlisted grades, officers, and junior enlisted Marines. The origin of the term is naval.

HEAD. Bathroom, toilet, restroom, or latrine (odious to Marines because it is an Army term). When 3rd Battalion, 2nd Marines, attended Jungle Warfare School in Panama, an Army installation, they spent part of the first day there replacing all signs saying "latrine" with signs saying "head."

HOOTCH. Anything from a tent to a wooden hut. A poncho stretched between two trees as a primitive rain shelter is also a hootch.

IRISH PENNANTS. Loose thread or fiber on a uniform.

JUNK ON THE BUNK. During inspection, a Marine lays out all his gear and uniforms (junk) on a flat surface, such as his bunk.

K-BAR. A Marine's fighting knife.

LPH, LSD, LPD, LCU, LST. Acronyms designating a variety of landing ships that the U.S. Navy uses to transport Marines. An LPH (Landing Platform, Helicopter) is a large carrier capable of transporting 2,000 Marines and 24 helicopters. An LSD (Landing Ship, Dock) is a large amphibious ship that can conduct a "controlled sinking" by filling its well deck with water, enabling the landing craft to float out. An LPD (Landing Platform, Dock) is a combination of an LPH and an LSD. An LCU (Landing Craft, Utility) is a small landing craft frequently transported inside an LSD. An LST (Landing Ship, Tank) is a small landing craft capable of carrying as many as three battle tanks. LSTs may also be transported inside the belly of an LSD.

LVTP. Landing Vehicle Tracked Personnel — the correct military designation for an amtrac, a large, clumsy, but efficient armored personnel carrier that is amphibious. Current models will carry some 20 Marines plus a three-man crew. LVTC designates a Command vehicle, loaded with radios and other communications gear.

LIBERTY. In the early days of the Corps, "liberty"

meant the time Marines were allowed ashore in a home or foreign port. The term still applies, although now, liberty also describes a night on the town. Liberty is limited time off, usually one or two nights, which differentiates it from "leave," where time off is more extended.

MCAS. Marine Corps Air Station.

MEU. Marine Expeditionary Unit. The smallest air-ground task force, normally built around a reinforced infantry battalion and a composite aircraft squadron.

MOS. Military Occupational Specialty, or a Marine's primary training. For instance, 03 stands for infantry, 02 would be intelligence, and 08 would be artillery.

MRE. "Meal, Ready to Eat." Supplanting the C-ration cans of the "Old Corps" are lightweight plastic packets of dehydrated food.

MAGGIE'S DRAWERS. A complete miss on a firing range announced by a big red flag.

MARINE BARRACKS. The buildings where Marines guarding a naval base live. Today, Marine Barracks are also found in Washington, D.C., (the original Marine Barracks) and elsewhere, far from any naval base.

MESS HALL. Building where Marines eat.

MIKE BOAT. The smallest landing craft in Navy inventory; also known as an LMC. A typical LMC can carry 25 Marines.

MORNING COLORS. The colors of the United States of America are hoisted every morning at 8 o'clock at all Marine installations around the world. In the evening, colors coincide with sunset.

MOUNT OUT. Getting started, leaving an area, going ashore during a landing.

MUSTANG. An enlisted man or woman who has obtained an officer's commission.

OCS. Officer Candidate School, a boot camp for young men and women who want to become Marine officers. Located in Quantico, Virginia, OCS is one of the toughest schools in the Marine Corps.

OLD CORPS. Everything was always better in the "Old Corps." The Old Corps ended just before a more junior Marine entered the Corps.

POLICE. Cleaning up an area, such as a bivouac. To "police an area" or organize "police detail" has nothing to do with law enforcement.

QUARTERDECK. The main deck of a ship or the main level of a building.

RECON. Reconnaissance Marines are organized in three active-duty battalions and one reserve battalion. Their primary job is to obtain pre-landing and post-landing intelligence by being inserted into enemy territory. They like to think of themselves as the toughest men in the Corps, the elite of the elite.

REQUEST MAST. Old naval term describing a Marine's right to request an interview with his commanding officer.

SACK. Another term for bunk, rack, or bed.

SALTY. Having seen and done much in the Corps. Being "salty" is almost as admirable as having served in the "Old Corps." Young Marines will go to great lengths to get the "salty" look, including dropping their helmets repeatedly on rocky ground. The rocks scuff and tear the helmet camouflage, making it look old and well used.

SCUTTLEBUTT. Rumor. Initially, the term meant a water fountain, where rumors presumably originate and spread.

SECURE. Finishing up work. "I will secure at 1600," means a Marine will shut down his work at 4 p.m. and go home.

SHIP OVER. Marine lingo for reenlisting. "Ship for six" means to reenlist for another six years.

SLOPCHUTE. Any business establishment that serves beer.

SNAPPING IN. This term originates in boot camp where Marine recruits do hours of dry runs with their rifles, learning the basic shooting positions, how to aim properly, how to reload, how to take the rifle apart and, blind-folded, how to put it back together, naming each part. The term is used by Marines to indicate that they are new at a job and are still learning it.

SQUARED AWAY. Someone or something that makes a good impression. "Squared away" refers to a smart, well-maintained uniform or a successful exercise involving a large number of Marines.

STARBOARD/PORT. Naval terms for right and left, respectively.

SURVEY. To exchange faulty equipment for new gear, or to leave the Corps under less-than-honorable circumstances.

TOP. A Marine master sergeant, one of the senior staff NCO ranks.

TOPSIDE. On dry land, topside indicates the top floor or the roof of a building; aboard ship it refers to the top deck.

TROUSERS. Pants are always referred to as "trousers" in the Marine Corps. Use of terms like "trousers" or "blouse" is traditional in the Corps; misuse earns push-ups or other penalty exercises in boot camp.

TUNA BOAT. Tank drivers' term for amtracs fully loaded with Marines.

UTILITIES. What most civilians and the Army call "fatigues."

782 GEAR. The equipment a Marine carries in the field, including web belt, suspenders, ammunition pouches, canteens, first-aid kit, pack, helmet, entrenching tool, poncho, and poncho liner. The term originates with the form used in the "Old Corps" that listed the items issued to a Marine. The form was number 782. Marines who are (or want to be considered) "salty" will refer to the equipment as "deuce-gear."

U.S. MARINE CORPS CHRONOLOGY

ROYAL MARINES

The Lord High Admiral's Regiment, also known as the Duke of York and Albany's Maritime Regiment of Foot, was raised in 1664 by King Charles II. This force, frequently disbanded when hostilities ceased and reestablished when war resumed, was to become known as the Royal Marines.

The statement, "Tell it to the Marines," is attributed to King Charles, who made the comment when a naval captain, after a long cruise, reported to the king that he had seen flying fish. The king was doubtful, but the colonel of the Royal Marines, Sir William Killigren, confirmed the sighting. Apparently, the king then believed the story. Turning to Secretary of the Admiralty Samuel Pepys, he said, "No class of our subjects hath such knowledge of odd things on land and sea as the Marines. Hereafter, when we hear a yarn that lacketh likelihood, we will tell it to the Marines. If they believe it, then we shall know it is true."

Royal Marines have fought side by side with U.S. Marines several times — during the Boxer Rebellion in China (1900) and in Korea (1950-53), for example. Today, the two Corps often train together.

Their emblems are surprisingly similar; each has a globe — the U.S. Marines' depicts the western hemisphere and the Royal Marines' the eastern hemisphere. "If you put the two Corps together," quipped a Royal Marine sergeant major during maneuvers in Norway, "we own the world."

GOOCH'S MARINES

For England's war with Spain, the American Colonies in 1740 raised four battalions of Marines designated as the 43rd Regiment of Foot to serve with Admiral Edward Vernon's fleet. These 3,000 men, commanded by the governor of Virginia, Colonel William Gooch, were known as "Gooch's Marines." In July 1741, they landed at Guantanamo (then known as Walthenham Bay), Cuba, to secure a base for the British Fleet. Today, U.S. Marines guard that same base, which was acquired by the United States during the Spanish-American War.

MARINE CORPS BIRTHDAY

The U.S. Marine Corps, first called the Continental Marines, was established on November 10, 1775, by the Continental Congress at a meeting in Philadelphia, Pennsylvania. The Congress proposed to raise two battalions of men who were "good seamen, or so acquainted with maritime affairs as to be able to serve to advantage by sea, when required." The owner of a nearby tavern, Samuel Nicholas, was named commandant of the Continental Marines on November 28, 1775. He is considered to be the first Marine Corps commandant. Although undocumented, legend has it that Tun Tavern served as a recruiting station for the Marine Corps.

FIRST AMPHIBIOUS LANDING

The Continental Marines participated in the first major operation of the Continental Navy on March 3, 1776. Eight small U.S. ships with 12 officers and 234 enlisted Marines raided New Providence in the Bahamas to capture gunpowder badly needed by George Washington's troops.

(Facing) Drum Major uniform, Drum and Bugle Corps, Marine Barracks, Washington, D.C.

WAR OF INDEPENDENCE

Three types of Marines served in this war: Continental or Regular Marines, which were raised by the Continental Congress; Marines of the State Navies; and Marines of the privateers. Highly disorganized and plagued by money, supply, and recruiting problems, Marines participated in many actions, including the Second Battle of Trenton (January 2, 1777). The Marines, along with the Continental Navy, disappeared by the war's end.

REESTABLISHING THE CORPS

When the first Congress assembled in New York in 1789, the U.S. had neither Navy nor Marines. On July 11, 1798, Congress passed a law forming a Corps of Marines. On the same day, Congress also authorized the establishment of the Marine Band.

The new commandant of the reestablished Corps, Lieutenant Colonel William Ward Burrows, first located his headquarters in Philadelphia; then in 1800, he moved to Washington, D.C., where new Marine Barracks at 8th and I Streets were completed in 1806.

THE SHORES OF TRIPOLI

The war against the Bashaw of Tripoli—which concerned the right of American merchant ships to sail the Mediterranean—started in 1801. A famous incident of that war involved the American consul at Tunis, William Eaton, and Marine Lieutenant Presley N. O'Bannon. In 1805, with a force of nine sailors and Marines, 40 Greeks, a squadron of Arab cavalry, 100 Turks and other mercenaries, and a caravan of camels, Eaton and O'Bannon marched across 600 miles of Lybian desert and seized the port and town of Derne near Tripoli. Presley N. O'Bannon was awarded a Mameluke sword by the Viceroy of Egypt. This sword served as the pattern for the "Mameluke sword," which is carried by Marine officers to this day.

WAR OF 1812

Marines participated in several actions of the war, including the Battles of Bladensburg and New Orleans. The new Marine Barracks and the commandant's house were among the few buildings not burned by the British when they occupied Washington.

DECADES OF PEACE

After the War of 1812, three decades of peace followed, and the Marine Corps, like the rest of the armed forces, shrank. In 1817, just 14 officers and 652 enlisted men were on the rolls of the Corps. In 1820, Congress appointed Archibald Henderson as commandant. He had joined the Corps in 1806 and was commandant for 39 years (1820-1859), serving under 11 presidents and rising to the rank of brigadier general.

THE HALLS OF MONTEZUMA

Marines served in all actions of the Mexican War, both ashore and afloat. In 1847, Marines played a crucial role in the attack and seizure of Chapultepec and Mexico City. The citizens of Washington later presented Commandant Archibald Henderson with a blue-and-gold standard which bore the motto, "From Tripoli to the Halls of Montezuma."

Marines drill in hollow square formation on fantail of U.S.S. *Kentucky*, ca. 1900.

Peking Legation Guard undergoes troop inspection, ca. 1910.

EVERY CLIME AND PLACE

Marines served with Navy ships throughout the world, supporting U.S. foreign policy, and protecting U.S. citizens and their properties. They saw service, for instance, with the East India Squadron. Commanded by Commodore Matthew C. Perry, the squadron went to Japan on March 31, 1854, to open the country up for trade. The senior Marine aboard was Major Jacob Zeilin, later to become commandant.

CIVIL WAR

Marines, quickly mobilized at the barracks at 8th and I Streets in Washington, participated in quelling the uprising at Harper's Ferry in 1859. They later participated in many actions of the Civil War, but never became a major force. On January 1, 1861, the total strength of the Corps was just 1,892 men and officers. Some officers resigned to join the South and served in the Marine Corps of the Confederacy, which at its peak, counted 600 men.

SPANISH-AMERICAN WAR

The Corps demonstrated again its value in seizing and defending advanced naval bases. In June 1898, after a quick mobilization, Marines landed in Guantanamo Bay, for the second time in 160 years. Today, Marines form the first line of defense for this U.S. base.

CHINA

During the Boxer Rebellion in 1900, Marines achieved fame defending the Legations Quarter in Peking. Embassy duty was still rare in those days, but the spirited Marine action during the rebellion firmly established that role for the Corps in the American mind. (To the distress of the Corps, a U.S. Army detachment temporarily took over guarding the Peking legation when, right after the Boxer Rebellion, the Marines were shipped off to fight the Moros in the Philippines.) The role of the Corps as embassy guards was formally established in 1948.

Marines also served with the multinational force that included Royal Marines, Italian Marines (Battaglione San Marco), German Naval Infantry, and others, who, under German command, had come to China to relieve the foreigners at Peking. In Beirut in 1982-1984, the Italian Marine Corps served as part of the multinational force stationed there. During a dinner "celebrating" the first year of the Multinationals in Beirut, the commandant of the Italian force pointed out to his groaning officers that "the last time Italian Marines served along with U.S. Marines, they ended up staying for 40 years."

Elements of the 4th Marines would serve in Shanghai as late as 1941. The long period in China was to have a lasting influence on the Corps. The phrase "Gung Ho" (Chinese for "working together" or "work in harmony") was brought into the Marine Corps by Brigadier General Evans F. Carlson, who served in China during the 1930s with the Marine Detachment at Peiping, and later as a military observer with the Chinese forces.

Marines gather in sand trenches near Vera Cruz, Mexico, ca. 1914.

SUPPORT OF FOREIGN POLICY

In the years 1900-1914, the Corps was often the "Big Stick" employed by Washington to carry out foreign policy. Marines quelled disturbances or helped stabilize friendly regimes in Nicaragua (Marines landed in 1910 after having been required to land there seven times before to help protect U.S. citizens and property), Panama (1901, 1902, 1903), Honduras and Dominican Republic (1903), Cuba (1906, 1912), Dominican Republic (1912-1924), Mexico (1914), and Haiti (1914-1918).

MARINE AVIATION

First Lieutenant Alfred A. Cunningham gave Marine aviation its official start when he reported for duty at Annapolis, Maryland, on May 22, 1912. Marine aviators saw their first combat in France during World War I.

(Above) Marines on bicycle patrol served as messengers of the Signal Battalion prior to World War I. (Below) Officer stands in special full-dress uniform, ca. 1912.

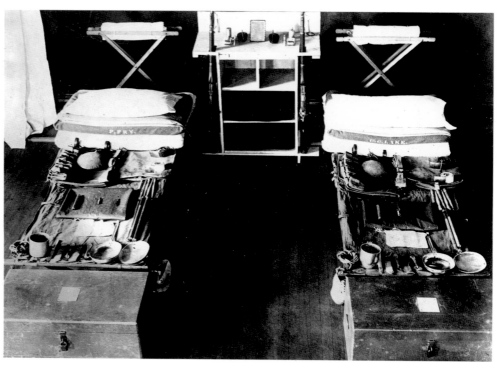

(Above) Recruits' equipment, ca. 1914. (Below) Signal detachment
of the Advance Base Force, 1916.

Funeral procession in Brooklyn, New York, on May 11, 1914, for Marines killed in action in Vera Cruz, Mexico.

WORLD WAR I

For the previous 25 years, the Corps had been an expeditionary force, relinquishing its more traditional role of providing sharpshooters and guards aboard ships. In the many wars in Central America, China, and the Philippines, the Corps started to operate as a fully equipped land force gathering vital combat experience.

When the U.S. entered World War I in April 1917, the Corps numbered just 14,000 men and officers, but rapidly expanded to include 75,101 men and, for the first time, women, in its ranks by the end of the war. Two Marine brigades were dispatched to France. The 4th Marine Brigade served in the U.S. Army's 2nd "Indian Head" Division, successfully clearing well-entrenched German troops from Belleau Wood. Marines also served in major battles at Chateau Thierry and in the Argonne. More intensive fighting followed for the brigade, which was cited three times in French Army Orders.

The 5th Marine Brigade served in France mainly as military police and support units, since the American Expeditionary Force commander, General John Pershing, refused to permit the Marines to establish a separate division. General John A. Lejeune (later to become one of the most influential Marine Corps commandants) was the first Marine to command an Army division.

General Lejeune and staff review combat exercises of the 2nd Battalion, 5th Regiment, in Germany.

Marines board a troop transport during the early 1920s.

Flag-draped caskets returning World War I dead from overseas are lined up in the Brooklyn Naval Yard, January 1921.

(Above) Marine stands watch over the Rhine, ca. 1918. (Below) Combat training of 1st Battalion, 6th Marines, in the snow-covered fields in Germany.

BANANA WARS

Between the World Wars, the Corps served in numerous small conflicts, most of them in Nicaragua, Haiti, and the Dominican Republic. These long, protracted engagements with guerrilla forces helped the Corps formulate a doctrine for small wars. The *Small Wars Manual,* written in the 1930s, became a foundation for further study of Marine Corps operations in localized conflicts.

As innovators, the U.S. Marine Corps developed concepts that have been credited with much of the success of the U.S. Pacific campaign during World War II. The Corps refined amphibious landing techniques and defined its role in seizing amphibious bases, while Marine aviators experimented with the techniques of dive-bombing and the concept of close-air support.

(Above) Marines survey damage to the American Legation following the 1931 earthquake in Managua, Nicaragua. (Below) Captain "Uncle Joe" Pendleton at the capture of Coyotepe Hill, Nicaragua.

WORLD WAR II

Guadalcanal, Saipan, Tarawa, Iwo Jima, Okinawa —in the American mind, the Corps became associated with certain victory thanks to its island-hopping campaign, which proved to be the recipe for victory in the Pacific. The Corps grew from just 54,000 members in June 1941, to 485,000 men and women at the end of the war, with six divisions and four aircraft wings (plus numerous separate ground units and air squadrons).

Marines are pinned down on the beach at Namur in the Marshall Islands, February 1, 1944.

(Above) Marines salvage ammunition from cases that broke open while being brought ashore to Saipan, July 3, 1944. (Facing) F4U Corsairs of the "Hell's Belles" USMC fighter squadron are silhouetted against the sky by anti-aircraft fire during a Japanese air raid on Yontan Airfield, Okinawa, April 16, 1945.

Two Marine privates hit the deck to throw a scorching inferno at
the defenses that blocked the way to Iwo Jima's Mount Suribachi,
February 24, 1945.

(Above) A squad of riflemen maneuvers in Iceland during the winter of 1941. (Below) A Marine of the 2nd Battalion, 27th Marines, who won the Navy Cross for leading a charge on the bloody beach at Tarawa, checks his rifle after 10 days on the front lines of Iwo Jima, March 1, 1945.

Two Marines on the wings of an F4U Corsair.

(Above) A Marine heads for Iwo Jima's beach in a Higgins boat on D-day, February 24, 1945. (Below) More than 200 pounds of fresh "gizmo" fish are inspected by members of the 4th Marine Air Wing stationed on the Marshall Islands, 1944.

Tank-led U.S. Marines accept the surrender of enemy troops on
Wolmi Island, Korea, as a tank commander points out another pillbox,
September 15, 1950.

KOREA

Hastily mobilized when the Korean War started, the Corps served with distinction during the three-year engagement. With the amphibious landing at Inchon in September 1950, the Corps' 1st Marine Division helped establish a second front in Korea. Later in the war, the Corps fought a major battle against Chinese forces at the Chosin Reservoir. During the Korean War, the Corps applied the innovative concept known as "vertical envelopment," a tactic combining traditional overland troop movements with troop deployment by helicopter. The Corps had pioneered this technique in the late '40s.

RESCUING THE CORPS

Following World War II, there were strong pressures exerted, endorsed by President Harry S. Truman, for unification of the U.S. armed forces under a single Department of War. Between 1946 and 1952, the Marine Corps was in danger of being drastically reduced in size and mission. The Corps, threatened with relegation to a level of junior partner in the defense establishment (President Truman called it a "landing party that got out of hand"), had no seat on the Joint Chiefs of Staff. The Corps did not get voting rights until 1978. Louis A. Johnson, who followed James Forrestal as Secretary of Defense in 1948, cut the Corps to just eight infantry battalions and 12 aircraft squadrons, and forbade the official observance of the Marine Corps birthday.

The role of the Marines was ensured following the dramatic landing at Inchon, Korea, in September 1950. In 1952, Congress passed a law reaffirming the Corps as a separate service with three divisions and aircraft wings, plus one reserve division and aircraft wing. This ordinance, known as Public Law 416, also clearly defined the Corps' role.

Marines move through the streets of Seoul, Korea, in the early 1950s.

(Above) Marines serving in Korea with an infantry company of the 2nd Battalion, 1st Marine Regiment, prepare for a night patrol deep into Chinese Communist territory, December 1, 1952. (Below) A Marine is rushed from a jeep ambulance to a helicopter, which will take him to a rear-area hospital. Helicopter evacuation of front-line casualties saved thousands of lives in Korea.

GLOBAL SUPPORT

At the end of the Korean War, the Corps returned to its duties of providing support for U.S. foreign policy. These duties now included having a force permanently deployed in the Mediterranean Ocean. In 1958, the Corps landed a peace-keeping force in Lebanon, and in 1965, returned to the Dominican Republic to help quiet disturbances there.

VIETNAM

Vietnam was the longest war the Corps has ever fought. In charge of the I Corps area, which constituted the northern third of South Vietnam, the Marines participated in many of the operations of the conflict, losing more than 13,000 troops killed in action. After the initial landing in Vietnam in 1965, the role of the Corps in the war went beyond its predominant mission of amphibious warfare.

(Above) Members of the 1st Reconnaissance Battalion demonstrate the extraction procedure employed in densely canopied areas in the Republic of Vietnam, May 22, 1969. (Facing) Marines of 2nd Platoon, Company I, 3rd Battalion, 9th Marines, smoke out a suspected Viet Cong cave during Operation Skull, October 16, 1965.

(Above) A tank driver with Company C, 1st Tank Battalion, scans the muddy road while providing security for a convoy near Da Nang, Vietnam, October 1967. (Facing) Marines carry a fallen comrade killed by Viet Cong forces during Operation Union II in the Tam Ky area of South Vietnam, May 30, 1967.

A Marine from the escort ship U.S.S. *Harold E. Holt* (DE-1074)
searches the merchant ship S.S. *Mayaquez*, captured by Cambodians
in Koh Tang, Cambodia, 1975.

LEBANON AND GRENADA

In 1983, the Marines participated in the Grenada intervention. During the same period (1982-1984), Marines were also used in an attempt to serve a "peace-keeping" role in Lebanon. This second Marine deployment in Lebanon led to disaster in October 1983, when 241 Marines and sailors were killed in a suicide attack by an Iranian-backed Shiite terrorist, who drove a truck loaded with explosives into the Marine compound.

TODAY

The U.S. Marine Corps supports American foreign policy worldwide, whether in northern Norway, the Indian Ocean, or the corridors of the U.S. Embassy in Paris. All over the globe, Marines are serving. "Semper Fidelis."

In Beirut, Lebanon, a Marine remains concealed behind a sandbagged barricade while studying the surrounding territory with an M-65 battery commander's telescope. Marines were deployed in Lebanon as part of a multinational peacekeeping force in 1983.

Photographs on pages 171-172, 174-182, top photograph 187, and 188 printed courtesy of the National Archives; on pages 183-186, bottom photograph 187, 189-190, and 192-199 printed courtesy of the U.S. Department of Defense, Still Media Records Center.

Wings on the Wind

BIRD POEMS

COLLECTED AND ILLUSTRATED BY
KATE KIESLER

CLARION BOOKS
NEW YORK

Clarion Books
a Houghton Mifflin Company imprint
215 Park Avenue South, New York, NY 10003
Copyright © 2002 by Kate Kiesler

The illustrations were executed in oil paint.
The text was set in 13-point Adobe Caslon.
Book design by Janet Pedersen.

www.houghtonmifflinbooks.com

Printed in Singapore

Library of Congress Cataloging-in-Publication Data
Wings on the wind : bird poems / collected and illustrated by Kate Kiesler. • p.   cm. • Summary: A collection of
serious and humorous poems about birds by such authors as Eleanor Farjeon, Carl Sandburg, and Edward Lear. •
ISBN 0-618-13333-X • 1. Birds—Juvenile poetry. 2. Children's poetry, American. 3. Children's poetry, English.
[1. Birds—Poetry. 2. American poetry—Collections. 3. English poetry—Collections.]
I. Kiesler, Kate. • PS595.B54 W56 2002 • 811.008'03628—dc21 • 2001037103

TWP 10 9 8 7 6 5 4 3 2 1

*Grateful acknowledgment is made to the following for permission
to reprint the copyrighted material listed below:*

"Those Crazy Crows" from *Nibble, Nibble* by Margaret Wise Brown. Copyright © 1959 by William
R. Scott, Inc., renewed 1987 by Roberta Brown Rauch. Used by permission of HarperCollins
Publishers. • "The Swallows" and "Go Southward, Birds!" from *Summer Green* by Elizabeth
Coatsworth. Copyright 1948 Macmillan Publishing Company, renewed 1976 Elizabeth Coatsworth
Beston. Reprinted by permission of Simon & Schuster Books for Young Readers, an imprint of
Simon & Schuster Children's Publishing Division. • "House Hunters" by Eleanor Farjeon.
Copyright 1933, 1961 by Eleanor Farjeon. Reprinted by permission of Harold Ober Associates
Incorporated. • "Something Told the Wild Geese" from *Branches Green* by Rachel Field.
Copyright 1934 Macmillan Publishing Company, renewed 1962 Arthur S. Pederson. Reprinted by
permission of Simon & Schuster Books for Young Readers, an imprint of Simon & Schuster
Children's Publishing Division. • "Gretchen's Parakeet" by Kristine O'Connell George. Used by
permission of the author, who controls all rights. • "One Blackbird" by Harold Monro and "The
Barn-Swallow" by William Sargent from *Rainbow in the Sky* by Louis Untermeyer. Published by
arrangement with the Estate of Louis Untermeyer, Norma Anchin Untermeyer c/o Professional
Publishing Services Company. • "The Woodpecker" by Elizabeth Madox Roberts from *Under the
Tree* by Ivor S. Roberts. Copyright 1922 by B. W. Huebsch, Inc., renewed 1950 by Ivor S. Roberts.
Copyright 1930 by Viking Penguin, renewed 1958 by Ivor S. Roberts & Viking Penguin. Used by
permission of Viking Penguin, a division of Penguin Putnam Inc. • "Look at Six Eggs," an excerpt
from "Prairie" from *Cornhuskers* by Carl Sandburg. Copyright 1918 by Holt, Rinehart and Winston,
renewed 1946 by Carl Sandburg. Reprinted by permission of Harcourt, Inc.

For Cheryl,

whose letters are always filled

with the flap and flutter of birds

from *House Hunters*

ELEANOR FARJEON

Birds will be house-hunting
Soon—think of that!
Crows in the elm-tops
And larks on the flat,
Owls in the belfry
And wren in the leaves,
And swifts will go house-hunting
Under the eaves.

5

One Blackbird

Harold Monro

The stars must make an awful noise
In whirling round the sky;
Yet somehow I can't even hear
Their loudest song or sigh.

So it is wonderful to think
One blackbird can outsing
The voice of all the swarming stars
On any day in Spring.

Sure

ANONYMOUS

When spring came whistling in,
    I heard a brown-bird hum,
As he sat on a bare oak branch,
    "I knew it would come—come.
    I knew spring would come."

The Barn-Swallow

WILLIAM SARGENT

In the Allegheny Mountains
    When the apple orchards bloom
I know of eaves in a big red barn
    Where I'll find nesting room.

I'm coming back! I'm coming back!
    My wings are on the wind;
I'm coming back with the spring-time
    To the hills I've left behind.

I'm coming back! I'm coming back!
    To the hills that I know best,
Where the mountains sleep, and the winds walk,
    And where my wings can rest.

The Secret

ANONYMOUS

We have a secret, just we three,
The robin, and I, and the sweet cherry tree;
The bird told the tree, and the tree told me,
And nobody knows it but just us three.

But of course the robin knows it best,
Because he built the—I shan't tell the rest;
And laid the four little—something in it—
I'm afraid I shall tell it every minute.

But if the tree and the robin don't peep,
I'll try my best the secret to keep;
Though I know when the little birds fly about
Then the whole secret will be out.

11

Look at Six Eggs

CARL SANDBURG

Look at six eggs
In a mockingbird's nest.

Listen to six mockingbirds
Flinging follies of O-be-joyful
Over the marshes and uplands.

Look at songs
Hidden in eggs.

The Little Birds

ANONYMOUS

The little birds sit in their nest and beg,
All mouth that once had been all egg.

13

Mrs. Hen

TRADITIONAL

Chook, chook, chook, chook, chook,
Good morning, Mrs. Hen.
How many chickens have you got?
Madam, I've got ten.
Four of them are yellow,
And four of them are brown,
And two of them are speckled,
The nicest in the town.

14

15

Time to Rise

ROBERT LOUIS STEVENSON

A birdie with a yellow bill
Hopped upon the window sill,
Cocked his shining eye and said:
"Ain't you 'shamed, you sleepy-head!"

The Swallows

ELIZABETH COATSWORTH

Nine swallows sat on a telephone wire:
"Teeter, teeter," and then they were still,
all facing one way, with the sun like a fire
along their blue shoulders, and hot on each bill.
But they sat there so quietly, all of the nine,
that I almost forgot they were swallows at all.
They seemed more like clothespins left out on the line
when the wash is just dried, and the first raindrops fall.

The Woodpecker

ELIZABETH MADOX ROBERTS

The woodpecker pecked out a little round hole
And made him a house in the telephone pole.

One day when I watched he poked out his head,
And he had on a hood and a collar of red.

When the streams of rain pour out of the sky,
And the sparkles of lightning go flashing by,

And the big, big wheels of thunder roll,
He can snuggle back in the telephone pole.

Misunderstanding

LEE BLAIR

A bird was singing
     "Chee-chee-chee."
He seemed to be
     Inviting me
To join him in
     The apple tree.

I climbed as I
     Had thought he meant.
He flapped his wings
     And off he went.
I've thought about
     The incident.

I climbed as quickly
     As I could.
The bird flew off
     Into the wood.
What was it
     I misunderstood?

To the Magpie

TRADITIONAL

Magpie, magpie, flutter and flee,
Turn up your tail and good luck come to me.

One for sorrow, two for joy,
Three for a girl, four for a boy,
Five for silver, six for gold,
Seven for a secret ne'er to be told.

Five Little Owls

ANONYMOUS

Five little owls in the old elm tree
Fluffy and puffy as owls could be,
Blinking and winking with big round eyes
At the big round moon that hung in the skies.
As I passed beneath, I could hear one say,
"There'll be mouse for supper, there will today."
Then all of them hooted "Tu-whit, Tu-whoo!
Yes, mouse for supper, Hoo hoo. Hoo hoo!"

The Herons on Bo Island

ELIZABETH SHANE

The herons on Bo Island
        Stand solemnly all day;
Like lean old men together
        They hump their shoulders grey.
Oh, I wish I could get near them
        To hear the things they say!

They turn up their coat collars
        And stand so gloomily;
And somehow, as I watch them,
        It always seems to me
That in their trouser pockets
        Their wrinkled hands must be.

But if I venture near them
    They look at me in doubt,
And with great wings loose-flapping
    They circle round about,
Their long legs hanging downwards,
    Their slim necks all stretched out.

If I stood on Bo Island
    As gloomily as they,
And ruffled up my collar
    And hid my hands away,
It might be they would join me
    And I'd hear the things they say.

27

The Parrot

ANONYMOUS

I am the pirate's parrot,
I sail the seven seas
And sleep inside the crow's nest.
Don't look for me in trees!

I am the pirate's parrot,
A bird both brave and bold.
I guard the captain's treasure
And count his hoard of gold.

from *The Sandpiper*

CELIA THAXTER

Across the lonely beach we flit,
  One little sandpiper and I;
And fast I gather, bit by bit,
  The scattered driftwood, bleached and dry.
The wild waves reach their hands for it,
  The wild wind raves, the tide runs high,
As up and down the beach we flit—
  One little sandpiper and I.

Above our heads the sullen clouds
     Scud black and swift across the sky;
Like silent ghosts in misty shrouds
     Stand out the white lighthouses high.
Almost as far as eye can reach
     I see the close-reefed vessels fly,
As fast we flit along the beach—
     One little sandpiper and I.

I watch him as he skims along
     Uttering his sweet and mournful cry;
He starts not at my fitful song
     Or flash of fluttering drapery.
He has no thought of any wrong,
     He scans me with a fearless eye;
Staunch friends are we, well-tried and strong,
     The little sandpiper and I.

from *The Pelican Chorus*

EDWARD LEAR

King and Queen of the Pelicans we;
No other birds so grand we see!
None but we have feet like fins!
With lovely leathery throats and chins!
    Ploffskin, Pluffskin, Pelican jee!
    We think no Birds so happy as we!
    Plumpskin, Ploshkin, Pelican jill!
    We think so then, and we thought so still!

We live on the Nile. The Nile we love.
By night we sleep on the cliffs above;
By day we fish, and at eve we stand
On long bare islands of yellow sand.
And when the sun sinks slowly down
And the great rock walls grow dark and brown,
Where the purple river rolls fast and dim
And the Ivory Ibis starlike skim,
Wing to wing we dance around,—
Stamping our feet with a flumpy sound,—
Opening our mouths as Pelicans ought,
And this is the song we nightly snort;—
    Ploffskin, Pluffskin, Pelican jee!
    We think no Birds so happy as we!
    Plumpskin, Ploshkin, Pelican jill!
    We think so then, and we thought so still!

Gretchen's Parakeet

KRISTINE O'CONNELL GEORGE

Gretchen's parakeet—

    sitting on her shiny flute,
    tipping his head,
    listening to scales.

Gretchen's parakeet—

    sitting on his silver branch,
    suddenly singing
    his own song.

Those Crazy Crows

MARGARET WISE BROWN

Those crazy crows on ragged wing
Fly over the woods
They never sing
They screech and they scream
But they never sing
Those crazy crows
They never sing.

Something Told the Wild Geese

RACHEL FIELD

Something told the wild geese
    It was time to go.
Though the fields lay golden,
Something whispered, "Snow."
Leaves were green and stirring,
    Berries, luster-glossed,
But beneath warm feathers
    Something cautioned, "Frost."
All the sagging orchards
    Steamed with amber spice,
But each wild breast stiffened
    At remembered ice.
Something told the wild geese
    It was time to fly—
Summer sun was on their wings,
    Winter in their cry.

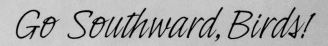

Go Southward, Birds!

ELIZABETH COATSWORTH

Clap hands! clap wings!
go southward, birds!
The winter's near
with snow like curds,
and frost whose touch
is strange and light—
seek your hot suns
with wings and flight!

Clap hands! clap wings!
why linger here?
The snow will drift,
the winds blow drear.
Go! robin, bluebird,
wren and swallow!
Fly! fly ahead!
and we will follow!

Birds in the Garden

ANONYMOUS

Greedy little sparrow,
    Great big crow,
Saucy little tom-tits
    All in a row.

Are you very hungry,
    No place to go?
Come and eat my breadcrumbs,
    In the snow.